OPEN HEARTS

Renewing Relationships *&* With Recovery, Romance & Reality

Gentle Path
P R E S S

ALSO BY PATRICK CARNES, PH.D.

Contrary to Love: Helping the Sexual Addict
Don't Call It Love: Recovery From Sexual Addiction
A Gentle Path Through the Twelve Steps
Out of the Shadows: Understanding Sexual Addiction
The Betrayal Bond: Breaking Free of Exploitive Relationships
Sexual Anorexia: Overcoming Sexual Self-Hatred
  (with Joseph M. Moriarity)

ALSO BY MARK LAASER, PH.D.

Before the Fall
Faithful and True
Talking to Your Children About Sex

OPEN HEARTS

Renewing Relationships With Recovery, Romance & Reality

PATRICK CARNES, PH.D.

DEBRA LAASER

MARK LAASER, PH.D.

Gentle Path
PRESS

WICKENBURG, ARIZONA

GENTLE PATH PRESS
P.O. Box 3345
Wickenburg, AZ 85358
www.gentlepath.com
800-955-9853

First Edition

Library of Congress Cataloging-in-Publication Data
Carnes, Patrick; Laaser, Debra; Laaser, Mark
    Open Hearts: Renewing Relationships With
Recovery, Romance & Reality/Patrick Carnes, Debra
Laaser, Mark Laaser—1st ed.
p. cm.
Includes bibliographical references.
ISBN 1-929866-00-3
1. Couples. 2. Relationships 3. 12-step. 4. Recovery

Design by Theresa Gedig
Set in Berling

Printed in the United States of America

Dedicated to Judy Weedman, who has been an inspiration to us all

Acknowledgments

The authors acknowledge the hard work of Joe Moriarity, who worked with us to develop the initial manuscript in 1994. We also wish to thank the current board of the National Council for Couple and Family Recovery for its commitment to making *Open Hearts* available to everyone. Two board members, Carol and Dennis Birke, labored many hours to complete the preparation for publishing. We have deep gratitude to all the couples who completed NCCFR's We Came to Believe programs. Their pioneering spirit helped refine the exercises, which make up the heart of *Open Hearts: Renewing Relationships With Recovery, Romance & Reality.*

Who needs this book?

Couples in troubled relationships often have these characteristic beliefs. Look over this list and note which ideas you believe are true about yourself, and which you think hold true for your partner.

STINKING THINKING
Typical beliefs in unhealthy relationships
1. Being together and unhappy is safer than being alone.
2. It is safer to be with other people than to be alone and intimate with my partner.
3. If I let my partner know who I really am, what I've done or what I'm feeling, he or she will leave me.
4. It is easier to hide and medicate my feelings through addictive/compulsive behavior than to express them.
5. Being caught up and totally dependent on each other is seen as being in love.
6. We find it difficult to ask for what we need, both individually and as a couple.
7. Being sexual is equal to being intimate.
8. We either avoid our problems, or feel we are individually responsible for solving them.
9. We believe that we must agree on everything.
10. We believe that we must enjoy the same things and have the same interests.
11. We believe that to be a good couple, we must be socially acceptable.
12. We have forgotten how to play together.
13. It is safer to get upset about little issues than to express our true feelings about larger ones.
14. It is easier to blame our partners than to accept our responsibility.
15. We deal with conflict by getting totally out of control or by not arguing at all.
16. We see ourselves as inadequate parents.
17. We are ashamed of ourselves as a couple.
18. We repeat patterns of dysfunction from our families of origin.

If you and your partner identify with any of these, this book is for you.
Open Hearts will help couples
- who are struggling in their relationship, regardless of the reasons
- whether or not addiction is involved
- regardless of the legal status of their relationship
- regardless of their sexual orientation.

Whatever your situation, *Open Hearts* can work for you.

Table of Contents

A Word of Hope

Some of you have tried many times to fix your relationship. Others of you are new to your first serious commitment. Or perhaps you've been in unhealthy situations in the past and hope to make this one work.

We understand your struggle because we've been there.

We know what it's like to have trouble with communication, parenting, finances and sex. We know what it means to feel discouraged or hopeless about the future of your relationship, and even ashamed about yourselves as a couple. We understand how you got to this point.

This workbook describes a series of exercises to help couples use the strength and hope of the Twelve Steps to heal a struggling relationship and create a healthy one. You need not be familiar with the Twelve Steps or part of a 12-step recovery group to make this process work for you. Any couple wanting to build healthy and fulfilling intimacy will benefit from this book.

Begin this healing process by giving yourself the credit you deserve for being a survivor. You grew up and coped. You did the best that you could with what you had. And your parents did, too. Recognize that you didn't have the modeling, the instruction or the unconditional love and nurturing you deserved as you were growing up. You lacked the tools to have a healthy relationship—and that's exactly what this book gives you.

The strength of this program, like any 12-step fellowship, is that it depends on people helping people—in this case, couples helping couples. You are not at this point because you are wonderfully wise, or an academic who understands the clinical and theoretical issues at hand. You are reading this book because you have struggled with many of these issues yourselves. Your strength is your experience.

Note: Throughout the book, we have used pronouns interchangeably to avoid the burdensome use of "she or he." Relationship problems know no gender bias.

First developed by Alcoholics Anonymous founder Bill W. to help compulsive drinkers gain sobriety and serenity, the Twelve Steps have evolved into spiritual principles applied in other addictions and all areas of human growth. Though you may at first shy away from their association with addiction, in *Open Hearts*, you'll see how the Steps offer profound revelations about ourselves and our relationships.

No matter the degree of difficulty or dysfunction you're experiencing in your relationship, there is always hope. We encourage you to trust this process. The principles set forth in Open Hearts have helped thousands of couples.

Take heart—this is a gentle path to help you work through your problems and renew your relationship.

Authors' Notes

What did guerrilla warfare in the jungles of Central America have to do with my marriage in the late 1970s ... aside from the emotional bombshells, verbal ambushes and self-righteous sniping?

Actually, my wife and I became involved with a movement called base communities that originated in the Catholic Church in the '70s during the terrible strife in Central America. Originally designed to bring families together in the face of overwhelming adversity, it had been adapted with remarkable success to succor families on the frontlines of our fast-paced, superstressed technological culture.

What I liked most was belonging to a committed group of couples. I found a level of warmth and support unlike anything I had experienced previously, even beyond 12-step and therapy experiences.

Unfortunately that group dissolved with a leadership change in the parish, as did the marriage a few years later. I found myself a single parent with four children for more than a decade. However I never forgot the laughter, joy and camaraderie that I found with that group. There were many nights when I wondered if things might have been different if we had stayed in that wonderful community.

People tell me

recovery improves

dramatically when

there is a couple

component to their

program.

In the late 1980s, I was working at Golden Valley Health Center in Minnesota and proposed a retreat series for couples based on the Twelve Steps. As a family therapist, I had been struck by how the Steps were an ideal tool to intervene with a dysfunctional family system. Couples often feel powerless as the dysfunctions of the family system repeat, no matter how hard the partners try to stop. That systemic momentum paralleled what addicts and codependents experience as individuals. Resonating behind the conceptual ideas for me was the memory of the healing power of the base community of couples I had experienced.

The program that emerged was called We Came to Believe–Mark and Deb Laaser were among the first participants. When some of these early We Came to Believe couples recognized their need for community, they started Recovering Couples Anonymous, now a worldwide fellowship with meetings in most areas of the United States. Many of the We Came to Believe principles and materials were adopted by RCA and used in the book *Recovering Couples Anonymous*.

The strength of the RCA program became clear to me when researching *Don't Call It Love*, a study of 1,000 recovering sex addicts. The couples who put together the strongest recoveries had 12-step couple support such as RCA. To this day, people tell me that recovery improves dramatically when there is a couple component to their program.

Now, in support of the work of the National Council for Couple and Family Recovery, an outgrowth of RCA dedicated to helping families cope with addiction, we are making those ideas more available through *Open Hearts*. This book contains all the basic materials of the original We Came to Believe program, plus expanded exercises and background material.

Open Hearts: Renewing Relationships With Recovery, Romance & Reality helps couples initiate recovery *as partners*. Designed to be read together, it can be used as part of any self-help couples group. Plus, professionals now have a resource to integrate the principles into their couples services.

When living a 12-step way of life, we develop a reverence for the steps and the communities of people who choose to commit to that way of life. Over time we see miracles evolve which build faith in a power greater than ourselves. I consider *Open Hearts* to be one of them. Twenty years later the warmth of that initial base community still glows in my heart. In some ways the care of those people continues to radiate to others through this program and the wonderful people in RCA. I feel privileged to have witnessed it all.

Pat Carnes

Authors' Notes

This may shock you, but we don't have a perfect marriage.

Although we'd each gained tremendous help from the 12-step meetings we attended, we realized those meetings dealt with the problems of individuals–not couples. If one of us vented about a relationship issue, we received massive amounts of support for ourselves individually, which did little more than reinforce our self-righteous belief in our particular position.

This help was flawed because no one in our meetings heard our partner's side of the story. Since we lacked the help we needed for our problems as a couple, we were still dealing with strong feelings of loss, hurt and grief about our relationship. We often found ourselves fighting the same old battles.

We often found ourselves fighting the same old battles.

We then joined a therapist-led couples group where we finally were able to address our problems together–and to discover that we were not alone in our struggles. It was not until our participation in the We Came to Believe seminars, however, that we realized just how common our problems and concerns were.

We both know that this process has saved our relationship. We trust that for you, as for us, working through the Twelve Steps as a couple will be a gentle process, taken one day at a time, as you build greater commitment, caring and communication in your relationship.

Deb and Mark Laaser

Open Hearts *serves as the text for* We Came to Believe *programs held throughout the country. The process described here works best in a group of couples offering support and feedback.*

For information on We Came to Believe *programs, contact the National Council on Couple and Family Recovery at the address found on page 215. To locate a Recovering Couples Anonymous group in your area, call 314-830-2600, email rca@iname.com, or visit http://www.recovering-couples.org*

HOW: *Honest, Open and Willing*
A User's Guide for This Gentle Path to Healing

This book is divided into two main sections:

Part One forms the foundation of this workbook. It contains an explanation of the core principles needed to rebuild or create a relationship, and the background for working through the exercises found in Part Two.

In your desire to get to work on your relationship, you may be tempted to skip Part One and jump right into the exercises of Part Two. Please don't. Reading Part One is essential because you will better understand the factors that contributed to the current state of your relationship. In addition, Part One helps you see that you are not alone in the difficulties you are experiencing in your relationship.

Part Two contains individual and joint exercises to work through the 12-step process that has helped countless couples rebuild their relationships and live happier, more fulfilling lives.

"Take the first step in faith. You don't have to see the whole staircase, just take the first step."

Martin Luther King, Jr.

- Each Step has exercises and specific instructions for you to follow. Concentrate on each exercise and each Step; avoid looking ahead.
- Take as much time as you need to do each exercise and Step. This is not a race! Move ahead when you both feel comfortable doing so.
- If particular parts of the book become difficult for you, take a break. You may even want to take time to talk with a counselor or trusted friend to clarify an issue that has arisen for you, either individually or as a couple.
- If you find yourselves having difficulty communicating or working through a particular exercise or section, it may mean one or both of you has an individual problem for which you need to seek help individually. If so, do so before trying to move on in the workbook.
- Because you are asked often to write, you each may want to have your own workbook. If you do so, designate one workbook as a common one where your joint work will be done.
- Be gentle with yourselves.
- During the 12-step process, you will find points at which you have made dramatic progress in your relationship. At these times, it's not unusual for couples to be tempted to quit the process because they think their relationship is healed. Don't–while these breakthrough moments are cause for celebration, they are only a beginning. The Twelve Steps are a complete package, and must be worked through from start to finish. If you abandon the process, your problems will likely return.

The Serenity Prayer

God, grant us the serenity
To accept the things we cannot change
The courage to change the things we can
And the wisdom to know the difference.

Prayer adapted for first We Came to Believe weekend
October 1988

PART I

Chapter 1: *Sharing Our Stories*

Before you begin to explore your relationship, before you rebuild health and intimacy, you need to understand the history of the family you came from–your family of origin.

Each couple's family stories are called their family "epics." Your histories help you understand how you found one another. Often, they act as the basis for your habitual and unconscious ways of interacting with each other. Your family epics form the foundation on which you begin your work.

Here are some other couples' family epics.

Power struggle

Kevin and Andrea have been married for 15 years and have two children. Kevin is a successful businessman, Andrea manages her own accounting business.

When Kevin was young, his mother and father didn't have a close relationship. His dad, a high-achieving professional, drank too much, and it wasn't unusual for him to shout at and even hit Kevin and his sister. At other times in his loneliness, Kevin's father turned to him as his main source of emotional support. As a child, Kevin took on the job of trying to ameliorate his father's emotional and physical loneliness.

Kevin's mother, if she was at all aware of these problems, seemed oblivious to them. And although she provided domestic support for the family, she was emotionally unavailable to both the children and their father.

As the daughter of a successful businessman, Andrea grew up in a home where money was never a problem. Though professionally trained, her mother gave up her career to take care of the family. On the surface, Andrea's family seemed warm and friendly, however, there was never a discussion or acknowledgment of emotions at any level. Andrea grew up lonely, feeling like a lost and unloved child.

Kevin and Andrea first met in college. Their relationship became one in which they focused primarily on pleasing each other to the exclusion of nurturing or caring for any of their own needs. On the surface, their relationship seemed selfless, but in reality, neither of them had any idea how to get any of their needs–physical, emotional, mental, or spiritual–met in the relationship.

Seven years into their marriage, just after the birth of their first child, Kevin's drinking became more frequent. He secretly blamed Andrea for never having time for him because she was always busy with kids or work, and he began an affair.

To Andrea, Kevin was becoming more withdrawn and emotionally unavailable. She responded by growing more involved in their children's lives and in her business. While she was unaware of Kevin's affair, she was troubled by his drinking and the growing distance in their relationship. Frustrated, Andrea didn't know how to talk about her feelings with Kevin.

Both Kevin and Andrea came from families in which parents and children had trouble expressing and understanding their emotions. Now, as adults in a relationship, they were encountering the strains all of us experience living with another person. Such stresses can be worked out with good communication, but only worsen if not addressed.

Both Kevin and Andrea sensed something was wrong in their relationship, but neither knew what to do about it. Their answer to this circumstance is common to couples whose relationships are in trouble: The partners either blame one another for the problems, or ignore them altogether and turn elsewhere to get their needs met.

Kevin and Andrea came to a We Came to Believe workshop on the verge of divorce. Constant fighting and drinking were problems in their relationship. Both felt hopeless and desperate, yet they were unwilling to let go of their relationship, in particular because of their children. It was a last-ditch attempt to salvage their marriage.

Missing the connection

Gordon and Diane had similar family backgrounds. Gordon's family was stoic, seldom expressing emotions and preoccupied with TV and sports. When she was growing up, Diane lived in a family setting where there were numerous emotional put-downs so she learned to keep her distance emotionally from everyone else as a way to protect herself. Aside from TV and eating, her family spent little time interacting with one another.

After nine years of marriage, Diane and Gordon felt their relationship was stalled. They were quite occupied with the lives of their three children. Gordon was heavily involved in his work and volunteered for many community activities. Diane had a part-time business in their home and spent the little time she had left over with two close female friends.

As their relationship grew more distant, Diane withdrew from her husband. She slowly convinced herself that Gordon was the "sick" one, that she was the strong one,

Couples in trouble either blame one another for the problems, or ignore them altogether and turn elsewhere to get their needs met.

that she could handle the household and kids on her own. It seemed to her that life might actually be easier if Gordon simply wasn't around. Period.

They didn't know how to be appropriately angry with one another, or how to tell each other what they were really feeling. Neither knew how to be honest either with themselves or each other. Though never physically violent, they were emotionally abusive to each other. Gordon was generally withdrawn, but at times he would suddenly vent his frustrations on the children, shouting at them and punishing them severely over trivial matters.

Every six months or so, Gordon and Diane would go through an intense period of arguments. Eventually, Gordon, the more verbal of the two, would talk Diane into calming down, re-convince her that he loved her, and that they should stay together.

Gordon and Diane existed in a cycle of ever-increasing distance, and their lives now had little physical, sexual or emotional connection. Both secretly harbored the feelings that they had made a mistake in marrying one another. Diane had begun to wonder if the only solution was divorce.

When Gordon and Diane came to the We Came to Believe weekend, they had already tried marriage counseling several times. When their counselors tried to teach them about communication, they seemed to grasp the principles quickly but could never apply them to their relationship. They read books on relationship improvement, and even attended a workshop on the same subject. Nothing seemed to help. They wondered if the We Came to Believe weekend would turn out to be one more futile attempt to heal their relationship.

Perfect from the outside

John and René both came from families that seemed to be perfect–from the outside. Active in church and community, their families seemed like happy, typical middle Americans. Inside their families, however, little emotional warmth flourished.

John and René both learned that outward appearances were important, that success meant having money and living in a nice house in an affluent suburb, and that they should handle all their problems by themselves.

After meeting in professional school, John and René pursued their careers. Later they tried to blend child rearing with their successful work. They bought a new home in a new suburb, and seemed to have created an ideal relationship and family.

But both John and René felt bored with their relationship. They didn't seem to have much to talk about, their sex life had become monotonous and increasingly unfulfilling. Several years ago, René had an affair, though she ended it quickly. John spent lots of time and money on clothes, his kids and the house. Life had little meaning for either of them.

Don't compare your insides to other people's outsides.

AL-ANON SAYING

A gentle path to healing

When John and René, Gordon and Diane, and Andrea and Kevin came to one of our workshops, the future of their respective relationships was uncertain and frightening. The questions they were asking themselves may sound familiar to you.

- Did we make the right choice in choosing one another in the first place?
- Can we deal with our own individual problems?
- Can we find meaning in our lives, both individually and as a couple?
- Can we rebuild trust in each other and in our relationship?
- Can we find sexual satisfaction?
- Do we need to maintain our relationship in order to be faithful to our children?
- Can we experience emotional, spiritual and sexual intimacy together?
- Can we learn how to be more honest about our anger, loneliness and resentments with one another?
- Would we be wiser to separate and divorce, and to begin again with a new partner?

Can you see some of the similarities among couples who are struggling with their relationships? The next chapter describes six basic dynamics underlying the problems in troubled relationships.

Chapter 2: *The Six Dynamics of Troubled Relationships*

For many years Pat Carnes used an awareness exercise in his couples/family workshops. The following account of one couple's experience with that exercise is an excellent example of how as couples–and parents–we find yourselves caught in harmful patterns of interactions that we seem to have no power to control or stop.

"When I'm with someone else's family, why are we happier than when I'm with my own family?"

"We didn't know how to be intimate"

We had been sent by our counselor to one of Dr. Carnes' family workshops, along with a list of relationship skills she felt we needed to work on.

According to our counselor, we didn't know how to set limits for ourselves. We didn't know how to solve problems. We didn't know how to be intimate. We didn't know how to explain our feelings to each other, or to let others in our family know what needs we had. We didn't know how to listen to one another. We didn't know how to have fun. And…well, the list seemed endless. Our marriage was clearly in trouble.

Once the class was assembled, the children were told by Dr. Carnes to walk around the room and pick out new "brothers" and "sisters." Next, those new "siblings" were told to pick out new "parents" from the adults in the group.

Once in our new "families," Dr. Carnes gave us all an assignment. Each family was to spend an evening doing something we had ever done before: roller skating, going to a baseball game, kite flying. At first it seemed to be little more than a problem-solving exercise. But soon we realized it was much more–it was an exercise in self-discovery.

With other people's spouses and other people's children, we discovered that we in fact did know how to set limits, to have fun and to problem-solve. In fact, we could do everything our counselor said we didn't know how to do.

When we came back to the group, one of the kids asked, "Why is it that when I'm with someone else's family, and we're playing like a family, we are like a family—and we're happier than when I'm with my own family?"

The rest of us—the parents—sat back and said, "Why can't we be like this with the people we love the most, our own family members?"

Why could these people communicate, play and problem-solve in their new "families"—with relative or complete strangers—but not in their own family? It wasn't a matter of not knowing how.

The answer, which quickly became apparent to workshop participants, is that they—like so many couples—are caught in a family/relationship system that is not functioning well, one that is not fostering intimacy, communication, commitment and fulfillment for all involved. Do you feel this is true about your relationship?

That's why this book was written—to help couples free their relationships from unhealthy and unproductive behaviors and patterns that have seemed impossible to escape.

It is possible to break these cycles. First we need to understand six major dynamics that keep our relationships from growing and changing.

1. *Couples in troubled relationships struggle with a lack of support and need a recovery process for their relationship.*

It's hard to be a couple in our culture. There are many pressures working against relationships. Historically, people worked, ate, played and celebrated together. Compared to those times, there is little support for families in our culture.

Today, family members simply aren't together much. Our culture separates adults from one another, as well as from their children, for great portions of each day. In many couples both partners need to work to support the family. Dad goes here to work, Mom goes there, or one works in the home while the other works outside it. The kids go off to school and unless they are close in age, they won't even be at the same school. Everyone arrives home at dinner time (or later), exhausted. They may eat together, but many families have schedules that don't allow this. Then Mom and Dad scramble to do housework and other projects while the kids deal with homework—or everyone plops down on the couch to watch TV.

It doesn't take too long before family members really don't know much about each other's lives because they have few common experiences. And because intimacy is based on shared life experiences, many families have little intimacy.

Recent studies of typical American family life reveal an astounding fact. Voice-activated tape recorders set up in participants' homes monitored all the conversations in the household. The results showed that the average couple spent less than 27 minutes *a week* in any kind of intimate conversation.

This is also the first time in history that we've ever asked just two people to try

Because intimacy is based on shared life experiences, many families have little intimacy.

to raise children. Until recently, children learned the trades they would need for adult life within the context of families. They didn't leave their families for six to nine hours a day to go to school because learning happened at home. What's more, everyone in a town knew all the children who lived there–everyone knew everyone else, for that matter. If any one child was causing trouble, any adult would feel within his or her rights to discipline that child because they knew that individually and as a community, they had an investment in that child. This meant, too, that the pressure for raising children wasn't solely on their parents, as it is in our society.

Most people used to live within a few miles of their relatives. Today, it's not unusual to live hundreds or thousands of miles from extended family members. Consequently, relatives are not available to help with child rearing. The pressures of raising children, combined with other activities, make it hard for couples to find time for themselves. Our families are torn apart because they don't spend time together and because they do not live in true communities. Furthermore, in today's culture the idea of divorce is generally accepted and rarely counteracted by strong encouragement to stay together.

Can you see that your struggle as a couple isn't only about you? Much larger cultural, economic and social forces are also at work.

It takes two

Another discovery became clear: Individual emotional, mental and spiritual health in each partner will not ensure that a couple will create a healthy relationship.

We may have assumed that as each of us became healthier individually, our bond also would get stronger. Not necessarily. Individual health, in fact, can be troubling and divisive in a relationship. If one or both partners begin to change and become more independent, it may threaten the status quo of the partnership.

Both partners must first attend to their own problems and issues for a relationship to survive and become fulfilling. That may mean attending group meetings, seeing a counselor or taking whatever steps each needs to heal themselves.

Then the partners need to turn their attention to the collective identity known as their relationship. We learn to have healthy relationships by practicing–by being in a relationship and working on it.

As a couple, we might follow a 12-step program together, get counseling together, or take whatever steps we need to heal our relationship.

Recovering Couples Anonymous symbolizes this with a three-legged stool: you, me and us. Your health, my health, our health. Without any one of the legs, the stool topples.

Individual emotional, mental and spiritual health in each partner will not ensure a healthy relationship.

2. Couples in troubled relationships come from families in which relationships were likewise troubled.

Each partner in the relationship brings along his or her unique family history, or epic. We don't seek to judge or blame our families for the difficulties we're having in our current relationships. Instead, we seek to understand our family roots and dynamics. By so doing, we can gain a better understanding of the family models each of us brings to the relationship. In addition, we can better understand the dynamics involved as we try to blend our own family histories into a new family. This is called the "blending of the epics."

Each of us is on a life journey. When we join another person to create a couple, these individual journeys take on even greater importance as two people try to merge their different backgrounds.

Those individual journeys include each partner's family epic, adding to the complexity and difficulty of this merger. Every family is really a great, transgenerational story. It's the story of all the many individuals involved, of their personal struggles, their ways of interacting and expressing emotion, of their ways of loving, of arguing, of communicating and more.

"One day, I heard someone define 'insanity' as doing the same thing over and over again and expecting different results... Not long after that, I heard a similarly uncomfortable definition.

"'Sanity' was humorously described as 'what we get when we quit hoping for a better past.' How often did I secretly whisper to myself: 'if only...'"

Ann, Al-Anon member

Our family helps determine the kind of person we look for in a partner. We look for a partner who can help us resolve the problems we experienced when we were growing up. If we become more aware of our family history, we can become more aware of the reasons we are attracted to particular types of people.

Today in our culture many people have lost or forgotten parts of their story. They are missing part of their personal history. Recovery groups such as Alcoholics Anonymous, Overeaters Anonymous and others encourage individuals to discover and tell their stories. Partners need to go through this same process *together as a couple*. They need to tell their stories to each other to begin forming a joint story. When partners share this process, a new truth begins to emerge that is critical to the success of the relationship.

First we must discover what happened to us in our families—what were the ways we learned to deal with feelings, conflict, anger. Next we need to share that knowledge with each other. Then we can understand why we react to one another and others the way we do. Until we can do this, real communication and intimacy are not possible.

If two people are at different points in their journey, they can be mismatched. Individuals who haven't completed certain developmental tasks look to their partner to solve them. Kevin, for example, never felt as a child that his mother was there for him when he needed her. Now, as an adult living with Andrea, he was inappropriately directing this need for mothering onto her. Kevin was enmeshed in Andrea's life and expected her to be available to him in whatever way he wanted.

When couples try to solve these developmental issues through their partner, they are not only doomed to fail, but they create further problems. It just doesn't work.

Our workshops role-play a scenario that illustrates this problem clearly. A man from the audience comes up on stage, sits on a chair and pretends to be a boy reading a book. Another person plays the role of the boy's bored little sister. "Little sister" walks by and bumps him in the head with an elbow. Then she trips over her "brother's" leg, and says, "What are you doing?"

"I'm reading," he replies.

"Little sister" plops herself down on her "brother's" lap and says, "Well, I don't know how to read, teach me to read," and keeps on pestering him.

What's going to happen now? Of course, eventually he hits her, and then she goes running to her mother, crying. Mom is already angry at boys who bully, so she comes in and punishes the boy, who was just sitting there reading and minding his own business in the first place. Does this sound familiar?

Some marriages are based on this principle. The husband is engaged in various activities (career, community work, time with the kids), and the wife feels ignored. She is bored with her life, so she does things to provoke him and gain his attention. Finally, he can't handle the provocations anymore and does something outrageous, perhaps even striking her.

She runs off to her therapist, or her mother, or whomever, and says, "Look at what he did." The husband gets all the blame and feels ashamed.

Certainly, the husband reacted inappropriately by screaming at her and striking her. He acted out. His wife, however, is not an innocent party, either. She has a key part in this little play. The problem revolves around their individual issues, but it's also a relationship problem.

These two individuals first need to look at themselves and their upbringing for the roots of their behavior. Next they have to help each other understand that behavior. Then they need to create new behavior patterns within the context of their relationship.

Can you see the necessity of doing this work as a couple? By working together, a bigger truth reveals itself. Then you can understand each other and break out of the cycle of destructive behaviors.

> Individuals who haven't completed certain developmental tasks look to their partner to solve them.

---

3. *Both partners in troubled relationships suffer from codependency.*

When both partners come from families with numerous unhealthy behaviors, they enter their relationship emotionally depleted. Unfulfilled, they don't have a reservoir of positive feelings. They don't even recognize such feelings. Since they don't understand how to nurture themselves, they look instead to others for nurturing. In addition, they have little idea how to get such healthy nurturing from their partner because they never learned how to do so, either in their family or from others.

Each partner, then, looks to the other for the love, approval and nurturing they were never able to give to themselves or receive from others. This is an attempt by them to meet their own needs for approval through their relationship. The actions they take to get that love and approval are called *codependency*: what they do to get their partner's love, nurturing and approval, while at the same time ensuring that their partner won't leave them.

Each participant in such a relationship is codependent. In addition to unhealthy and unproductive behaviors, this often leads to feelings of shame. We feel as though we are no good, that we are not worthy of anyone's love, attention or respect–even though we desperately want these things. A large part of our lives is concerned with trying to erase this feeling of shame, and our behaviors are an attempt to "medicate" this situation. Our relationship becomes enmeshed because each is seeking from the other the approval we can't give ourselves.

Although we generally are not aware of it at a conscious level, each partner is deathly afraid that the other will leave the relationship. But at a visceral level, we understand the situation–we know something big is missing from our lives.

Codependency styles vary, and for this reason people can mistakenly think that only one partner is codependent. That is not the case; it takes two to do codependency! Codependency, regardless of how it is played out, is based on a need for the partner's approval, love and affirmation–and it includes a powerful underlying fear in both partners of losing the relationship. Frank's story is a good example of this situation.

Frank grew up in a home where his physically and verbally abusive alcoholic father was seldom home. Frank's mother, in the pain and loneliness of that relationship, expected Frank to be the man of the family, to be responsible, to meet her emotional needs and to nurture her.

Although the relationship never became sexual, it was emotionally incestuous. Frank's mother essentially divorced Frank's dad and married Frank emotionally. In the process, Frank learned that he had tremendous power over his mother's feelings, and that he needed to be protective and helpful to her.

When Frank grew up and met his current partner, he assumed that the only way

> Each partner looks to the other for the love, approval and nurturing they were never able to give to themselves.

to please her was to be a caregiver–to nurture her emotionally, to be physically present, to do things for her–just as he had done for his mother.

Frank neither thought about what he needed and wanted to receive from a relationship, nor did he know how to express his own feelings. All he knew was that the only way to be valuable to a female in a relationship was to be the hero.

Frank may look at his present relationship and say, "No, I'm not codependent because I'm not needy. I'm not one of these victim types who just seem to be anxious about his partner all the time." But underneath lies a profound fear that his partner will leave him unless he meets all her needs.

Frank's story typifies the **competency** style of codependency. He played the hero/saint, with the expectation that his wife would always love him as long as he could be this way.

There are other styles: A person who has grown up in an abusive family can be a needy, anxious and depressed **victim**. Victims will say to their partners, in a codependent way, "Well, you can never leave me because I'm just too fragile."

Still other codependents play the **enabler** game, in which they make themselves invaluable to their partner by doing everything they can for them. While one partner is out doing things, the other is taking care of the home front.

There is also the **sexual style**, in which one partner believes that if the other is kept sexually pleased, he/she will stay. If the partner always says yes to sex, it means he/she is liked.

Regardless of the style of the codependent relationship, both partners feel emotionally depleted. They don't know how to ask for nurturing, and they're still deathly afraid of losing their partner. Consequently, they continue manipulating one another rather than speaking openly and honestly.

> Although we are not aware of it at a conscious level, each partner is deathly afraid that the other will leave the relationship.

Approval from within, not without

Part of the challenge of improving your relationship is to figure out how you're manipulating your partner to gain approval. How are you seeking approval from without, rather than from within?

Before you begin working on Part Two with your partner, look individually at what you've been willing to do to maintain your partner's approval.

What roles do you play?

What do you do to keep your partner in the relationship? (The exercises in Part Two will help you accomplish this task.)

We need to understand that we can survive in the world without our partner, that it is possible for us to get our emotional, mental, physical and sexual needs met without our partner. These realizations allow us to make a decision to stay with our partner because we *want* to, not because we *need* to out of fear of living without him or her.

Now the need for individual recovery becomes clearly important. A relationship cannot and will not progress and improve if the partners individually remain unable to affirm themselves and find support for themselves outside their relationship.

> If you would like more information on codependency, the following books provide much insight.
>
> *Facing Co-Dependency*, Pia Mellody
> *The Betrayal Bond*, Patrick Carnes
> *Codependent No More*, Melody Beattie
> *Adult Children: The Secrets of Dysfunctional Families*, John Friel and Linda Friel
> *Is It Love or Is It Addiction*, Brenda Shaeffer

---

4. *Partners in troubled relationships have difficulty being intimate with each other.*

Intimacy means the mutual and honest expression of all parts of one's life: anger, worry, elation, sorrow and other emotions, as well as one's aspirations, dreams and doubts.

Partners in unhealthy relationships cannot be intimate with others. They cannot because they hold beliefs similar to the following:

"My partner is the person I've selected as the most likely to fulfill my needs for love and affection. She's also the person I'm most afraid of losing. But if she really knew me, she wouldn't really like me, and she'd want to leave me. So I don't dare tell her who I really am."

This way of thinking leads each partner to avoid bringing up problems and painful parts of their relationship–the very areas that must be dealt with openly if intimacy is ever to develop and the partnership is to survive. Where relationships most need honesty, they have dishonesty.

Both partners further assume that if the other person really loved them, that person would tell the truth. They both experience this lack of honesty as intentional lying and deceit. As a result, both withdraw, reveal even less about themselves and become more dishonest. Feelings of being abandoned by the other person grow, creating a dysfunctional, destructive cycle.

Many of the lies, manipulations and other secretive behaviors in dysfunctional relationships are really based on an inability to be intimate. As couples begin to heal, they must face this deep-rooted anxiety that says, "If I really reveal myself, my partner will hate me." This core belief must be overcome if there is to be a fulfilling relationship.

The process of learning to trust, to tell the truth, to be honest and self-revealing to your partner is incremental and slow. It takes practice. What's more, it is an ongoing experiment that tests whether or not you and your partner keep coming back as more is revealed.

Your partner's deceptions may be more a function of a fear of losing you than of a desire to deceive.

If you have experienced dishonesty from your partner, try to realize that it's not necessarily an indication that your partner doesn't love you. It may, in fact, stem from a deep love. Your partner simply doesn't know how to trust you intimately, and her deceptions are more a function of a fear of losing you than of a desire to deceive.

Healing depends on trust, and that means taking a risk. Trust means moving in a healthy direction–even if that is away from each other. One of the most profound paradoxes of recovery is that in order to get your relationship back, in order for it to be healthy, you have to be willing to risk losing it completely. As a couple, you have nothing left to lose, and nowhere to go but up.

Couples who have actually been in the lawyer's office preparing for a divorce may have an easier time recovering because they came to the point where they admitted the possibility of being apart. They have actually faced the loss of the relationship. Couples who have never reached this point must at some time accept that they are willing to lose their relationship. After all has been revealed, one partner may in fact decide to leave. Being honest is more important than anything else. To find intimacy, both partners must surrender.

"I'd been in a self-destruct cycle for so long, I mean those neuron pathways are etched into myself, and it makes it very difficult to live any other way. It makes it hard to let go and to have space and fill myself up with good things."

Sunny, recovering sex addict

And here lie the seeds of Step One: "We admitted we were powerless over our relationship and that our life together has become unmanageable." Step One calls on us to admit that no amount of dishonesty, verbal manipulation or other attempts at control have had (or will ever have) the power to fix and save our relationship.

5. *Couples in troubled relationships suffer from "coupleshame."*

Living in the midst of the cycle described in Dynamic No. 4 *(Partners in troubled relationships have difficulty being intimate with each other)*, partners find that they aren't being honest with each other. Besides not communicating, they seem to either withdraw or fight. Any problem with money, their children or their social life only serves as further evidence that they and their relationship are a terrible failure. These couples haven't had a source of support, they are operating with family-of-origin problems, and they struggle with intimacy and codependency–all of which leads to feelings of "coupleshame": a core feeling of inadequacy as a couple.

The Carrot Peeler

Abe and Meisha's experience shows just how powerfully individual and family-of-origin problems affect a relationship.

Abe and Meisha were sitting in their counselor's office. The night before they had literally beaten each other up, and Abe had suffered a broken nose.

Passive, quiet and reflective, Abe grew up in a peaceful family with a mother who dominated his life and a father who allowed himself to be completely controlled by his wife.

Meisha's father, a workaholic physician and perfectionist, pushed Meisha relentlessly, rarely complimenting her. Daily household tasks fell to then 10-year-old Meisha, who became her father's "wife" after her mother was hospitalized for a nervous breakdown.

Meisha eventually earned three master's degrees, a doctorate and a law degree. While professionally successful, she was perfectionistic, anxious, volatile and used Valium regularly.

Meisha complained regularly that Abe didn't help enough with the housework. The day before their counseling appointment, Abe decided he'd fix some dinner.

Abe was preparing tacos and had made a bit of a mess when Meisha arrived home. Once she began banging around in the kitchen to make a salad, Abe soon got the message that he wasn't wanted there anymore. He headed to the living room to watch the evening news.

Meisha wanted to peel a couple of carrots for the salad and reached into the drawer where the carrot peeler was usually kept. It wasn't there, and Meisha immediately assumed that since Abe was the last one to use the kitchen, he'd left it somewhere else. (It was in the dishwasher.)

Meisha headed into the living room, asking Abe where the peeler was.

Abe replied, "I didn't use it. I was making tacos."

Meisha didn't believe him. "Come on, tell me where the damn peeler is."

Feeling unappreciated and angry, Abe replied, "I don't know where the goddamn peeler is, and what's more, I don't give a damn where it is, either."

The exchanges continued, growing more heated. Abe finally decided that the only way to control his wife was to play John Wayne and slap her.

The hitting escalated until Meisha picked up a lamp and smashed Abe in the face. The battle stopped at this point only because Abe was bleeding all over one of Meisha's favorite rugs.

Now they found themselves sitting in the counselor's office, ashamed that their relationship had become so dysfunctional that they had actually come to blows over a carrot peeler.

Abe and Meisha both came from families where there was poor communication, where they received little emotional support, and where there were no healthy, intimate relationships.

As children, both Meisha and Abe had often blamed themselves for the troubles in their respective households. Now two extremely shameful adult individuals had formed a relationship without any idea how to nurture one another or themselves. Abe and Meisha were blind to the relationship patterns they were repeating, blind to the unfulfilled needs they had inherited from their childhood, and doomed to repeat this unhealthy and unfulfilling cycle. They were living in coupleshame.

Coupleshame closely parallels individual feelings of shame. Coupleshame appears when two individuals with core feelings of shame join in a relationship. As in mathematics, adding two negatives together makes an even greater negative. Two shame-filled individuals make a shame-based couple in which there is no possibility for a healthy relationship.

Destructive patterns

Sam and Paula had been going to Alcoholics Anonymous meetings for years. After divorcing from dysfunctional marriages after they began their recovery from alcohol addiction, they had avoided relationships for years out of fear of repeating their mistakes.

After meeting in AA, they married, but soon discovered that many of the same issues that had been part of their first relationships were surfacing again in this marriage. Unhappy, they began feeling like the marriage had been a mistake and that they'd chosen the wrong partner.

Both were saddened and disillusioned because they couldn't understand how, after all the work they'd done individually in their years of recovery and fellowship meetings, they could fall right back into the destructive patterns of their first marriages.

Paula and Sam's story exposes the harsh reality that merely making individual changes is not enough to give you the skills needed to create a fulfilling relationship. These skills can only be developed *in* a relationship.

When faced with a situation similar to Sam and Paula's, many couples reach the conclusion that they shouldn't be together and that they should divorce.

It is crucial to know that **you will not solve coupleshame through separation.** Nor will relationship difficulties and problems be solved by working separately outside of a relationship. If you do not work on your relationship issues in this relationship, you are doomed to repeat them in the next…and the next and the next. Couple recovery skills are just that: *couple* recovery skills. Although they parallel individual skills, you cannot work on them except in a relationship.

We learn to put down the weapons and pick up the tools.

AL-ANON SAYING

6. *Troubled relationships are a function of unhealthy development.*

In their relationships, couples go through stages of development, much as individuals do. They can also get stuck in a stage, unable to move beyond particular issues, arguments or fights. This can be frustrating and discouraging, to say the least.

If each partner is at a different relationship developmental stage, each will have different expectations for the relationship. Frustration mounts because neither meets the other's needs.

This book helps you recognize what developmental tasks you need to work on and what your relationship goals are. Couples say that it is a tremendous relief to finally understand why their relationship is stuck.

The following model is based on work by Ellyn Bader, Ph.D., and Peter T. Pearson, Ph.D., in their book *In Quest of the Mythical Mate.*

Addressing individual growth first, let's look at the six stages of child development from infancy through 3 years.

Stage 1. In this phase, infants are aware only of themselves, their immediate environment and the information they receive from their senses. They do not distinguish themselves from their environment.

Stage 2. Infants become aware of their primary parent. Their awareness of the immediate environment is totally dependent on identifying with their mother or father. All senses and needs are enmeshed with the parents.

Stage 3. Infants learn that their identity is separate from that of the parent. They have their own body, senses and needs.

Stage 4. Children who have learned to crawl are able to leave their parents. At first, this may only be to another room. They discover that they can exist on their own and alone, even if only for short periods of time. Being out of the eyesight of a parent is often frightening at first, but gradually a child feels safer and the length of time away increases.

Stage 5. Children come back to the parent to re-establish feelings of safety and for attachment. A child playing alone will periodically go to one parent just to see if they are still around.

Stage 6. Children learn and understand that they can come and go. They are experiencing independence and maintaining a relationship with the parent.

The skills needed to create a fulfilling relationship can only be developed in a relationship. You will not solve couple-shame through separation.

We flow in and out of these stages as we grow, expanding our exploration. We are seldom only working within one stage; often we are working on two or even three developmental tasks at once.

As a child grows older, for example, she or he feels safe enough to go to a friend's home for the night. Finally, children leave home completely to live independent lives.

If physical or emotional abuse occurs during one of the stages, a child may become stuck in that stage. In other words, in what is sometimes called developmental arrest, that stage's issues will not be learned and resolved.

As the child becomes an adult and enters relationships, arrested development can lead him or her to want a partner to help resolve these incomplete developmental tasks. For example, if a parent does not allow a child to learn independence by allowing him or her to come and go, the child can become emotionally enmeshed in the parent-child relationship. The child becomes stuck in Stage 2, never learning to be independent.

Couple's Developmental Stages

Let's turn now to the developmental stages in couple relationships. The process that a couple experiences in the growth and development of their relationship parallels the process children go through as individuals in their personal development. The level of development or maturity you reached as an individual affects the level you can reach in your relationships. Furthermore, if you've had problems at a certain individual developmental stage, your ability to work through the parallel couple stage will be compromised.

Stage 1. Self-centered
The world revolves solely around an individual's needs. Most often people in this stage are not in a relationship. If they are, they remain narcissistic and self-centered even in the relationship, which exists only to serve their needs. They do very little for their partner.

Stage 2. Discovery
In this discovery stage, oft-celebrated in romantic songs and poems, two individuals find each other. There is an excitement to this phase, a feeling so strong that it can be almost addictive. In this stage, each partner sees only the good in the other person. In what seems to be an ideal relationship, the partner is the dream lover and bells are chiming!

During this phase, the lovers don't seem to have needs of their own. Totally focused on each other, they spend massive amounts of time together, gazing longingly into each other's eyes, oblivious to the world. In love, they believe they have found the perfect partner with no faults.

Some people cannot move on from this phase, particularly if they are afraid that their partner will leave them if they express any negative feelings, thoughts or attitudes. Many people with such fears of abandonment create a mythical lover–a magic man or woman who will come along and resolve all their abandonment struggles. People stuck in this stage have not learned how to separate from others and cannot live truly independent lives.

Stage 3. Differences

During this phase, the partners discover differences in each other in such areas as politics, religion, personal habits, TV watching. They realize that the other is not the perfect partner they thought.

These newly discovered differences were always there; the partners were blind to them before. Healthy and mature individuals accept the reality that everyone has differences, it's normal, and that differences do not mean two people are not right for each other. In a healthy relationship, each partner can learn to listen, understand and accept the other, and still know that there does not have to be complete agreement at all times.

> "I can care about
>
> him, not for him."
>
> AL-ANON SAYING

Individuals who have not moved beyond this stage will struggle with disillusionment in their relationships. When the myth of the perfect mate is exploded, one or both partners can become hostile. These differences fuel many arguments, and can lead to anger, frustration and resentment. One or both partners may think that they haven't found the right partner and need a different one.

It is also in this stage that couples will acutely experience coupleshame. Unless the partners are recovering from their individual sense of shame, it is difficult to move beyond coupleshame.

Stage 4. Separate identities

The partners "leave" the relationship by going away from it to get some of their needs met. In a healthy relationship, partners understand that this is a phase in which they discover they don't need to depend totally on each other.

To accomplish this, both partners must know how to express their feelings and make healthy choices for themselves. They can have outside friends, interests, activities. They "practice" interpersonal skills with other interests and relationships in order to get some of their intimacy needs met.

People in unhealthy relationships do not know how to express their feelings in healthy ways. Nor do they know how to get their emotional, physical, sexual and spiritual needs met in healthy ways. They may, for example, turn to unhealthy escapes from their anger, sadness, fear and loneliness.

Many couples reach this stage only to find that their relationship has stalled. It is nearly impossible to get past this stage unless you individually have done the work necessary to be able to express your feelings and get your needs met in healthy ways.

Stage 5. Returning

This is the phase of coming and going. The partners learn that they can come back to the relationship to get some of their needs met. Their ability to do so assumes that they have skills in expressing feelings to their partner and in resolving conflict. If they don't, their efforts to come back will be met with the ongoing frustration of unresolved arguments and other problems.

In this phase, the partners no longer expect that the other will read their mind. They will ask for what they need. While they don't expect their partner to meet all of their needs, they can hear each other's feelings, including anger. They learn to fight fairly, avoid blaming and contract with each other for needs and expectations.

They don't depend on each other totally for emotional support. They have other healthy, meaningful relationships.

Stage 6. Healthy independence

In this stage, the partners know they have both a life together and a life apart. Each has his or her own likes, jobs, interests and friends, although some may overlap. Intimate, they are friends with one another. They meet many of each other's needs (sexuality, communication, child-raising, spirituality), though not all. They have a general interest in and concern for their partner's welfare. They are able to encourage and support their partner without fear of losing him or her. They also recognize that their life would go on if they were to lose their partner. Their choice to be together is a healthy, independent one.

Individuals who have not begun to resolve early abuse or developmental issues for themselves are unable to reach the later couple developmental stages. This is also true for couples who have not learned or practiced intimacy skills.

Chapter 3: *Family Systems*

In the previous chapter, you were introduced to the dynamics and beliefs of troubled or dysfunctional families. This chapter, focuses solely on the dynamics of family systems. It looks at how ineffective and unhealthy family systems affect partner relationships as well as other family members. Concepts introduced in this chapter form the foundation of much of the material and exercises in Part Two.

Setting boundaries

Healthy family systems are built around the cornerstone of healthy "boundaries." Think of boundaries as a kind of force field or safety barrier that surrounds us. Emotional and psychological health requires that we know how to set individual boundaries in times of emotional pressure. It also means that we know how not to set them when we want love and nurturing. We also need to know how to set reasonable limits–boundaries–for our relationship as a couple.

When we are children, we don't have the ability to set our own boundaries; it's up to our parents or primary caregivers to do so for us. As adults, parents know (or ought to know) how to protect, nurture and set boundaries for their children. By so doing, parents set an example for their children and teach them how to set boundaries for themselves. It is in this manner that ways of setting boundaries are learned and passed on from generation to generation.

Boundaries that are too loose

The way boundaries are set varies from family to family. In unhealthy families, parents sometimes set boundaries too loosely: Children are exposed to invasive abuse–physical, emotional, sexual or spiritual–and experiences from which they should be protected.

Physical invasion takes place when one or both parents physically abuse their children. These children may be struck, locked in their rooms, deprived of food, shouted at or threatened.

Emotional invasion takes place when a parent or other caregiver expects and teaches the child to attend to that adult's own emotional needs. For example: A father who loves tennis relentlessly pushes his boys into playing tennis because it makes him happy and because he wants to play with them.

Emotional invasion also occurs when an adult expects a level of understanding and support beyond a child's capabilities. For example, Dad's primary love is his work, so he is seldom home. Mom regularly says to her son: "I don't know what I'd do without you, Paul, you mean so much to me." Paul's mother has unfairly turned to her 9-year-old son for the understanding and emotional support which should be given by an adult.

Sexual invasion occurs in a variety of ways. It not only includes various forms of inappropriate touch, but may also occur when children are teased regularly about their bodies, when they're told inappropriate sexual jokes, or otherwise sexually harassed. It is important to note that if a child is living in an emotionally invasive relationship with a parent, then virtually any form of physical touching–kissing, hugging, lap-sitting–becomes erotically charged and is a form of sexual abuse.

Spiritual invasion occurs when, for example, children get messages from their parents that convince them they are a mistake in the eyes of God. (This discussion about spiritual abuse is not intended to make a theological statement, but merely recognizes that these behaviors exist.) For example, a 3-year-old slid down a banister one day only to fall off and bump her head. The child's mother responded by saying: "I wonder if Jesus wanted you sliding down that banister. If He did, I don't think He would have let you bump your head."

If any other forms of invasion take place by a religious authority, parochial school teacher or parent who's actively involved with a church, then by definition this also becomes spiritual invasion.

For more information about emotional abuse, see:

Emotional Incest Syndrome, Patricia Love
Silently Seduced, Kenneth Adams
The Verbally Abusive Relationship, Patricia Evans

Boundaries that are too rigid

Parents may also set boundaries too rigidly. In such cases, they create a shell around the child that overly insulates him or her from the surrounding world. Little can touch such children, including what ought to–love, care, physical affection and nurturing. Such children feel lost, abandoned and on their own.

Physical abandonment occurs when a child doesn't have a sense of physical safety (this may happen to latchkey children, for example), or when the parents leave their children for long periods of time. It also occurs when children receive little or no instructions on how to take care of themselves, such as when to go to bed, how to brush their teeth or how to eat right. Abandonment also occurs in situations where parents are physically present, but pay little or no attention to their children.

Emotional abandonment. If children are talked out of their feelings, they experience emotional abandonment. When a child comes to parents to talk about something upsetting and the parents say, "No, you're not upset; that was no big deal" or "Don't be sad," that is emotional abandonment. Though the child experiences feelings, the parents deny the existence or validity of these feelings.

Sexual abandonment occurs when the child does not receive appropriate modeling or instruction about healthy sexuality. For example: Parents who tell their daughter nothing about menstruation until she actually has her first period; parents who offer no support for their children for events which may be embarrassing (e.g., the first time they have to take a shower with other kids after gym class); and parents who do not teach their children about safe sex.

Spiritual abandonment occurs when a child does not receive modeling or instruction in healthy spirituality.

It's not unusual for the same child to experience both loose and rigid boundaries. One parent may create generally loose boundaries, while the other parent is setting rigid ones: A father regularly shouts at and puts down his children (a loose boundary), while the mother ignores this situation even when the kids go to her for help. The children are not being heard, protected, and nurtured as they should be (a rigid boundary).

Children may experience abuse in subtle and indirect ways: "Well, we don't expect you to be as good as your brother, because your brother is good at everything he does. He's just naturally smarter than you are."

Many adults who are struggling in their relationships grew up in families in which boundaries were either regularly violated or inconsistently set. As an adult, it is hard to set boundaries and build healthy relationships if one has never had a model for them.

Try to remember incidents of invasion or abandonment from your past. Let this process of remembering be gentle–your mind will allow you to remember incidents as you are able to deal with them.

Family system rules

In all families, members create rules of behavior. Often unwritten and unspoken, they guide the interactions of the family in many areas: what is talked about, how conflict is dealt with, how affection is expressed, how nurturing is given, how emotions are expressed.

Much tension is created in families who have unhealthy and inappropriate boundaries. Family members are in emotional (and sometimes physical) pain.

Unfortunately, however, they don't know how to deal with the tension and pain created by these boundary problems. In such families, the following five unhealthy rules are commonly created to allow family members to avoid dealing with tension and problems.

1. Don't talk.

The first rule in dysfunctional family systems is that no one talks about anything serious. The supposition is that if no one ever talks about anything serious, then no one will have to discuss the problems; therefore, the problems will go away. The "don't talk" rule has an equally damaging corollary belief: If someone in the family does talk about a problem, it will only make the problem worse.

2. Don't feel.

The second rule in dysfunctional family systems is "don't feel." Acknowledging any feelings is discouraged. Even such feelings as love and tenderness are frowned upon, because once family members acknowledge these feelings, other, threatening feelings such as anxiety, fear and anger will inevitably arise as well.

Family members try to belittle or deny feelings as best they can in a variety of ways: "Big boys or girls don't cry."

"Christians don't feel that way."

"God is going to make it better, so you don't need to feel that way."

"Get your act together."

"Get over it!"

"Everything will be okay in the morning."

Think back to your own upbringing. What were you taught about feelings?

If a problem does manage somehow to surface in a dysfunctional family and the don't talk/don't feel rules fail, then three additional rules come into play:

3. Denial.

Family members simply deny that any problem exists. They will counsel the offender with such comments as: "You're just imagining that" or "You're making too much of that" or "I don't see anything wrong, how in heaven's name did you come up with that idea?"

4. Minimizing.

If denial fails, then family members try to minimize the significance of the situation: "Yes, that's true, but it's no big deal," or "Other people have worse problems," or "Don't worry, things always work themselves out."

5. Blaming.

Finally, when all else fails, family members try to blame either a family member or persons, groups or situations outside the family. "If only X hadn't said X, then everything would be fine" or "He doesn't know what he's talking about, besides, he's always trying to make trouble."

Children living in families which operate with loose and rigid boundaries are being injured in a variety of ways, and the effects of these wounds often continue into their adult lives.

By living in a family where boundaries are routinely too rigid or too loose, children learn that the people they ought to be able to count on to meet their needs for care and nurturing are untrustworthy and unreliable. This situation confuses children because they no longer know whom they can trust.

As these children grow, they carry an ever-increasing pain of emotional injuries stemming from ongoing boundary violations. Eventually they begin to understand that something is not as it should be in their family. But when they try to raise these issues, the unhealthy family rules come into play.

This further compounds their problem because the rules force them to deny what they are experiencing and feeling. Not only have they already learned to distrust the adults in their lives, but they now are learning to distrust their own inner voice, too. They begin to doubt their ability to figure out what's happening to them. They no longer trust their own feelings. They feel pain, yet others tell them they aren't feeling it. They learn that it's not okay to express any feelings. They learn to avoid conflict. Eventually, they no longer recognize the pain they're carrying. The final result: They no longer trust themselves or others.

Family system roles

Members of dysfunctional families also develop roles designed to ensure that the household functions while burying underlying problems. These roles take the place of honest and open communication found in healthy families; they are, however, ineffective and ultimately destructive substitutes.

The following terms were created by Sharon Wegscheider-Cruse, whose writings include *The Family Trap, Understanding Me,* and *Another Chance: Hope and Health for the Alcoholic Family.*

- The **Hero** is the white knight, the person who's always right and always expected to solve things.
- The **Scapegoat** is the opposite of the Hero. Scapegoats are always seen as making mistakes or causing trouble.
- The **Mascot** is the comedian of the family. When family tension and pressure reach a certain point, the mascot will tell a joke or in some way try to diffuse the tension and deflect attention away from whatever is causing trouble.
- The **Lost Child** role develops at a very early age in children who have no one attending to their physical or emotional needs. Because no one listens to them, these children learn to give themselves the nurturing they need and want. They may spend an inordinate amount of time in their bedrooms, playing with imaginary friends to the near exclusion of real friends, watching TV, reading books, eating or playing Nintendo for hours–all to help them stay "lost." While all children take part in these activities sometimes, the Lost Child spends more

than normal time in such activities, and does so to avoid dealing with family life. They just disappear from family life, often receiving affirmation for never creating problems or making waves (a situation which creates tremendous inner turmoil in such Lost Children.) This inappropriate, unhealthy self-nurturing can contribute to addictive behaviors later in life.

- The **Enabler**'s job is to keep life running smoothly in the family so that problems don't surface. As a result, Enablers must tolerate the family's dysfunctional behavior, and when necessary, make excuses about such behavior, even to the point of lying to explain or cover it up. The Enabler acts as a kind of public relations coordinator for the family.
- The **Doer** is the task-oriented person in the family, the one who loves to get things done. Doers take care of the finances, they cook, clean, chauffeur the kids, do house maintenance, and so on. Doers often become workaholics in adulthood.
- The **Little Prince/Princess**–their role is to be cute, cuddly, a Shirley Temple/ Wally Cleaver type who never causes trouble. They try to bring out the sweetness in others by their own cute and sweet behavior.
- The **Saint** is the family member expected to carry the religious burden of the family. This role is sometimes combined with the Hero. Saints will go to church, Sunday school or even accept a religious vocation. Their responsibility (like the Hero's) is to always do the right thing, even if they don't feel like it.

Family members quickly become accustomed to the roles they are playing. Each member's self-esteem is dependent on the role he plays. While these roles may be hated, family members nevertheless understand that they need the roles for the system to maintain itself.

It is possible for an individual to play a combination of roles. A husband could be a Doer, a Hero and a Saint at different times. Similarly, more than one individual in a family can play the same role. As time passes, changes occur in who plays given roles, but the balance of the roles must always be maintained if conflict is to be avoided.

Ongoing family tension

Usually, dysfunctional families have numerous ways to deal with the tensions that inevitably arise in the course of living in an environment in which problems are never addressed.

The children grow up in what is called a "perpetual stress management seminar." If tension gets too high, someone will instruct them to watch TV, or fix them something to eat, or send them off to shop or play sports. It is not unusual for these behaviors to become actually addictive. These methods are the way families self-medicate to alleviate an ever-present and constantly simmering tension.

What kind of behaviors do you use to reduce tension and stress? How and where did you learn them? Are they healthy or unhealthy?

If either of you is healing from primary addictions (for example, alcoholism,

Generally, individuals choose a partner who plays opposite the role they learned while growing up.

eating disorders or gambling), in all likelihood there are other addicts in your family. Research has clearly indicated that addicts usually come from families in which other addictions are present.

Identify the addictions present in your family of origin.

It is crucial to begin recognizing the rules, roles and medicating behaviors you learned in your childhood. Generally, individuals try to choose a partner who will play opposite the role they learned while growing up. If you were a Hero or a Saint, you'll need a Doer or Enabler to take care of things while you're out riding your white stallion.

Deep wounds, deep shame

Abandonment and invasion cause deep wounds that can stay with children into their adult lives. Such wounds remain until they are consciously healed.

These wounds create anxiety, fear, sadness, loneliness, anger–but, above all, they create core feelings of shame. People with core shame think that the abuse they experienced was somehow *their* fault, that for some reason they deserved it. They believe that if they had just been better kids, they wouldn't have been abused.

Thus, shame stems from self-blame. These individuals learned in their families that they were bad; and they believed that if they weren't bad, they would have gotten the love they wanted and the safety they needed.

It is hard for children to recognize that the problems in their families are their parents' issues, not their own. Since children are seldom told differently, it makes perfect sense that they take on the blame.

People with a core of shameful feelings also believe they are worthless human beings. They believe that if they ever show others what they really think and feel, those people will find them unlikable and worthless. So rather than reveal their true self, something that's far too scary to do, shame-based people continually search for ways to manipulate others to gain approval.

This shame-based thinking denies the commitment of a friend (or a partner) to relationships, and perceives that a friend (or a partner) is lying about feelings and commitments. Shame-based thinking believes that even though others have said they care, they really don't. (Ironically, if shame-based individuals continue to be dishonest and manipulative, their friends will think badly of them.)

Feelings of shame and problems trusting others are deeply intertwined. Living with feelings of shame eventually erodes one's ability to trust others. Shame-based individuals don't accept that they'll be loved unconditionally. This belief stems from growing up in a family where there was abandonment and invasion, and where people did the opposite of what they said they were going to do. It is difficult to trust others if one has never seen and experienced trust-based relationships. For shame-based individuals, survival depends on not trusting. They learn to insulate themselves from others because if they don't, they will just kept getting hurt.

The decision to trust others can be scary. But you can choose to begin building trust with your partner. This process entails taking the risk to believe in your partner, to be intimate with your partner, to reveal yourself, and to find out, over time, that your partner will not take advantage of that honesty.

Work on yourselves

Can you see why you need to work both on your own issues and on your relationship? If you feel ashamed about who you are as a person, you must work to change this core belief. Only you can do so. To learn to trust another person, you must build the groundwork necessary to take that risk. You must learn to love, respect and trust yourself.

This two-faceted process forms one of the central themes of the 12-step process outlined in **Part Two** of this book: the need for *both* individual work and couple work. You alone can change your core feelings of shame to feelings of self-worth and self-esteem. Once you have done so, you can put them into practice in relationships with others.

Repeating cycles

Can you recognize also how the problems in your family of origin, the abuse you experienced, your arrested development, the roles and rules you learned for coping with the stress in your life, the dysfunctional or addictive habits you took up, and the shame you learned to feel about yourself are strongly related to the current state of your relationship?

In the following diagram, each partner has his or her own wheel of unhealthy, dysfunctional, and sometimes even addictive behaviors. In addition, the relationship also has its own separate wheel. The cogs on the wheels represent individual or couple problems and dysfunctional behaviors. As any particular wheel turns, it will engage and turn the other two. In the same way, the behaviors of either partner, or of the couple, will affect and drive the behaviors of the others.

COUPLE'S ADDICTION CYCLE

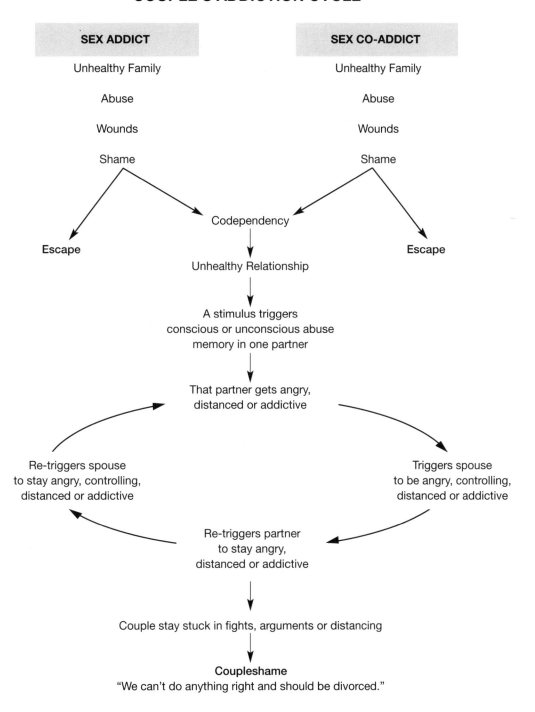

SEX ADDICT

Unhealthy Family

Abuse

Wounds

Shame

Escape

SEX CO-ADDICT

Unhealthy Family

Abuse

Wounds

Shame

Escape

Codependency

Unhealthy Relationship

A stimulus triggers
conscious or unconscious abuse
memory in one partner

That partner gets angry,
distanced or addictive

Re-triggers spouse
to stay angry, controlling,
distanced or addictive

Triggers spouse
to be angry, controlling,
distanced or addictive

Re-triggers partner
to stay angry,
distanced or addictive

Couple stay stuck in fights, arguments or distancing

Coupleshame
"We can't do anything right and should be divorced."

In a troubled relationship, both partners operate from a basic core of shame. Both have developed inappropriate or even addictive behaviors to deal with the challenges of their individual lives. When they become a couple, the partners blend their individual dysfunctional behaviors to create a new couple cycle in which these behaviors express themselves.

Many couple arguments and fights are intensified by this dynamic. Anger stemming from one partner's past family experiences, for example, might be projected onto the other partner, who is expected to alleviate it but can't. In other cases, one partner will say or do something that triggers family-of-origin memories in the other partner. These memories may have remained unconscious for years, but when triggered, they create a reaction not warranted by the current event, but which is consistent with the pain of old events. Past memories and behaviors have a tremendous power of their own. The wheels turn and turn.

Sam and Paula's experience (*see Chapter 2, page 15*) shows that creating a healthy relationship means not only stopping your own individual dysfunctional cycle, but your couple dysfunctional cycle, too. If you do not, it will continue triggering your individual cycles.

The challenge of change

If you recognize that even some of these core ideas are reflected in your relationship, ask yourself what you learned about your relationship by looking at your family of origin.

What led you to believe that you would be able to have a wonderful relationship with your partner?

Increased intimacy

As you begin **Part Two** of this book, you'll need to make a commitment to work on these exercises for a mutually agreed upon period of time. You are not asked for a "till death do us part" commitment. Still, you are asked to make a commitment to each other to work on your relationship for the next six to 12 months. During this time, promise not to make any final decisions about your relationship. Then, at the end of that period, agree to re-evaluate your commitment to this process.

You are urged to commit to this process, concentrate on the work in Part Two, and allow yourselves the freedom *not* to solve every issue. You are not working to create a finished product, a "perfect" couple. You are working to open up the process of communication and to give yourselves the tools for a lifetime of discovery, challenge and joy.

Progress, not perfection.

R e c o v e r y   s a y i n g

Will you encounter deep and intense emotions? Certainly, and your feelings will fluctuate throughout the process. You'll experience sadness, anger, anxiety, fear and even hopelessness, and you'll also feel joy, hope, serenity and peace.

It is important to understand that the ultimate goal of this process is not necessarily to keep partners together. The goal is to increase intimacy. Most often this will lead to increased or new commitment. Occasionally, it will lead to a healthy decision to separate. This is not failure. If the decision to be apart is based on healthy communication and mutual understanding, it is success.

Taking responsibility

This process will work only if you both are willing to take responsibility for the problems in your relationship. However, don't confuse this with taking responsibility for your partner's problems and struggles. Each of you is responsible for recovering from your own problems. Both of you, however, are mutually responsible for the problems in your relationship and for its relative health. You must let go of blaming and resentment before you can move ahead. Many of the exercises in Part Two are designed to reverse blaming.

A word of caution

If you find, as you get into this process, that it's leading to continual fighting, if it seems to make matters worse, then this may be because you still have *individual* issues that have yet to be adequately addressed and that are blocking your progress.

If this is true, be of good faith and have courage. It is suggested that you put your couple recovery on hold for the time being. Don't shelve it for good. Then get some help for your individual problems. Doing the needed individual work is part of your commitment to your relationship.

Comfort and joy

Finally, you are again welcomed to a journey of recovery as a couple. Whatever your background, whether you suffer from individual addictions or not, wherever you are in that hazy land somewhere between hope and despair, you are invited to apply these Twelve Steps to your relationship, and to trust in the Steps as a process.

Part Two uses the Twelve Steps as they have been adapted for couple work. This will be a gentle process for you. Those of you who have already used a 12-step program know how powerful these Steps can be in restoring sanity in the midst of chaos and despair.

Those of you who are unfamiliar with 12-step programs may be wondering how the short list of prescriptions that follows can possibly have any therapeutic effect. The Twelve Steps of Alcoholics Anonymous, which many, many people have used to successfully recover from a variety of addictions and dysfunctional behaviors, can also be used by couples to create healthier and more fulfilling relationships.

And take comfort in the words of The Promises in *Recovering Couples Anonymous.*

> *If we are honest about our commitment and painstaking about working the Twelve Steps together, we will quickly be amazed at how soon our love returns. We are going to know a new freedom and a new happiness. We will learn how to play and have fun together. As we experience mutual forgiveness, we will not regret the past nor wish to shut the door on it. Trust in each other will return. We will comprehend the word serenity, and we will know peace.*
>
> *No matter how close to brokenness we have come, we will see how our experiences can benefit others. That feeling of uselessness, shame and self-pity will disappear. We will lose interest in selfish things and gain interest in our partners, families, and others. Self-seeking will slip away. Our whole attitude and outlook on life will change. Fear of people and of economic insecurity will leave us. We will intuitively know how to handle situations which used to baffle us. We will be better parents, workers, helpers and friends. We will suddenly realize that God is doing for us what we could not do for ourselves.*
>
> *Are these extravagant promises? We think not. They are being fulfilled among us, sometimes quickly, sometimes slowly. They will always materialize if we work for them.*
>
> *… there are no problems that you have experienced that are not common to many of us.*
>
> *… the process of loving and communication grows in us and with each other one day at a time.*

New Rules for Relationships

Before you begin Part Two...

We recommend that you do not work Part Two of this book in isolation. One of the difficulties many of us have had in our relationships is a failure to admit to others that we need help.

You are encouraged to seek someone–a counselor, a clergyperson, a trusted individual or preferably another couple–who can witness your commitment to work through this process and help you when you need an impartial perspective.

This person or couple is called a sponsor or sponsor couple. Make an agreement to meet regularly, perhaps on a weekly basis, to review your work. Our experience tells us that being accountable to others adds dramatically to the success of this process.

Finding a sponsor

One of the great traditions that has grown out of the 12-step movement is sponsorship. A sponsor is another individual with more recovery and experience whom we ask to help us work through our own healing. We seek out someone who has what we want – serenity, wisdom, humor – or has walked a similar path. While this person may become a close friend, friendship is not a requirement for sponsorship.

We may feel awkward asking someone to be our sponsor. We may assume we are imposing and this may hold us back from reaching out for help. Overcoming these negative assumptions becomes a way of nurturing ourselves, a crucial first step in the road to our recovery.

Recovering couples have found that the following guidelines greatly enhance their ability to communicate.

1. It is okay to feel.

As you use this workbook, you may find that old and sometimes forgotten memories will surface. Some of you will be familiar with the emotions these memories elicit, but for others, this will be a new experience. There will be times when you'll feel anger, sadness or anxiety about the problems you are discussing. It is perfectly okay to feel the emotions that arise and to talk about them with each another.

Occasionally some of your feelings may seem stuck or blocked; in fact, one of your difficulties as a couple may be that one or both of you are not able to feel emotions. At other times, you may feel like your emotions are overwhelming.

Your work here may trigger the memory of some type of abuse you experienced in the past. If it does, an overwhelming feeling of sadness, anxiety or anger is likely to surface. As these memories and feelings surface, you are encouraged to take time out from the book and talk over your feelings with your partner or your sponsors.

You have permission to feel your emotions. Your body/mind will allow you to feel only the level of emotion you are capable of handling at any given time. You are encouraged not to judge each other's feelings. Your feelings are never right or wrong, they are simply your feelings–real for you at the time you are feeling them. Remember that it is always okay to feel.

2. It is okay to have conflicts.

At this point in your relationship, many of you have problems which you've been unable to resolve. Perhaps they remain unsolved because you've been unwilling to endure the conflict you knew would arise by facing them. Perhaps you have avoided arguments and fights of any kind.

Be assured that it's okay to fight. Later in the book, you will learn ways to fight in a healthy, safe manner.

If you reach a point where the conflict you're experiencing is getting out of control, you may need take a timeout and contact your sponsors. They can help you set limits so that the conflict doesn't become destructive to either one of you.

3. It is okay to have needs.

It's all right for you to have needs. It is okay, for example, to need your partner to listen to you or to help arrange for babysitting. Begin to recognize your needs, and begin expressing them to your partner.

This is not implying, however, that your relationship is at a point now (or that it ever will be) where you can expect your partner to have the ability to meet all your needs. No relationship can meet all your needs. There will always be some areas which have to be fulfilled in other places, regardless of the level of intimacy with your partner.

4. While using this workbook, you must respect your partner.

No self-righteous statements

Making self-righteous statements, such as declaring how wonderful you are, or how well you do things in comparison to your partner is discouraged. It is not fair to build points by putting your partner down. You are encouraged to begin looking at the times you blame your partner for the state of your relationship.

No baiting or button-pushing

By this point in your relationship, you are aware that certain things you do or say to each other will automatically create a reaction–for example, a statement that makes your partner cry or become angry. You are encouraged to begin identifying these "buttons" and stop pushing them.

No case-building

Many partners engage in what is called "case-building"–a recitation of past events which prove one partner's rationale for why the problems of the relationship are the other partner's fault. For example, if your partner forgot to give you a present on your birthday eight years ago, this incident should not be resurrected as an example of how she neglects you.

No taking each other's inventory

As another way of respecting your partner, please do not assess your partner's needs, feelings or problems. Avoid trying to gauge your partner's strengths, weaknesses or abilities. In 12-step lingo, this is called taking another person's inventory and it's a surefire way to double the discord. Try not to make assumptions or interpretations about your partner's family of origin. Your job in completing this workbook is to take only your own inventory, not your partner's.

5. Respect yourself.

Pay attention to what the little voice in your head is saying about you. Be aware of the times and ways you put yourself down–and stop doing so. Try to build yourself up by acknowledging your positive traits and actions.

Take responsibility for your story–the actions of your past

It is important for you to take responsibility for your story– your family, your actions (both positive and negative), your accomplishments and the consequences of your behavior.

No self-pity

Respecting yourself also means not indulging in self-pity. That means giving up feelings about how hard your life has been compared to others, how unfairly you've been treated.

Many of you who are victims of various types of abuse will recognize that it's easy to get stuck in the victim role. One way to know if you are stuck is that you experience ongoing anger. If this is the case, please seek the help of a therapist to help you move beyond feeling like a victim. It's difficult to have a relationship with your partner if you are continually blaming her for things that happened to you at the hands of others.

While your past certainly plays a role in your present life, it will be difficult for you to move ahead until you learn from your past and let it go.

6. What you say here, let it stay here.

As you work through this book, some of your discussions will be extremely sensitive. If you have close friendships outside this relationship, respect the anonymity of the process on which you are about to embark. Sharing your partner's story or the process that you are going through with a co-worker or friend is not appropriate.

This information must be kept confidential unless you give one another permission to share it. The sponsors you've chosen to help you work through this book may be privileged to some of these conversations, but even then you must both agree before either of you can divulge anything.

7. Rid yourself of expectations.

Finally, release specific expectations for how this process will work. It will take on a life of its own as you move into it. There is no set timetable for working through this workbook. No one is expected to work through the Twelve Steps in a few hours. You may work intensively for days or weeks at a time, and then back off for a while to digest what you have learned. At other times, you may need to seek individual help for issues that arise. Sometimes you might simply need a vacation from the intensity of the process. Conversely, you may find that you've gotten away from the process for a while, and that you need to re-commit to it. Don't criticize yourselves if it all seems to be taking longer than you had anticipated. Remember, there is no quick fix for relationships.

"Expectations are premeditated resentments."

Heard at an Al-Anon meeting

Slow is real, fast don't last

Above all, let this be a gentle process for you. Throughout the remainder of the book, you'll find our suggestions for taking "gentleness breaks"–time-outs for a walk in the park, reading an inspirational book, flying a kite with a child, watching a sunset.

Couple's Contract

We, the undersigned, agree to work on our relationship until _____

Date

We further agree not to make any final decisions about our relationship during this time.

_____   _____
Name   Name

_____   _____
Date   Date

We have signed this document in front of the undersigned witness(es), to whom we are accountable, and who have agreed to sponsor and be available to us as we work through this process.

_____   _____
Name   Name

_____   _____
Date   Date

Recovering Couples Anonymous
The Twelve Steps of RCA

Originally used by Alcoholics Anonymous to help people gain sobriety from alcohol, the Twelve Steps have since helped countless people recover from other unhealthy behaviors and addictions. While they address our relationship with God, they are spiritual, not religious, principles.

The Twelve Steps are simply a process and, as such, are a tool that can help people become more honest with themselves about who they are, where they've been in their lives, and what they need to do to lead more physically, emotionally and spiritually healthy lives.

Traditional 12-step meetings, however, are designed to work with individuals, not couples. Because of a belief in the importance of working *as couples* to rebuild relationships, a group of couples founded a new 12-step fellowship, Recovering Couples Anonymous. These couples wanted to help others use the Twelve Steps to rebuild their struggling relationships just as they had themselves. RCA revised the Twelve Steps to reflect the problems and concerns of couples. Just as the Twelve Steps have helped millions of individuals become healthier, these steps now can help couples who are struggling with their relationships in the same way.

Listen to how this program works, in words taken from *Recovering Couples Anonymous*, 3rd ed., p. 54.

Rarely have we seen a couple fail who has thoroughly followed our path. Those who do not recover are people who cannot or will not completely give themselves to this simple program. They are naturally incapable of grasping and developing a manner of living which demands mutual and rigorous honesty. There are those, too, who cannot or will not make a commitment to their partners. There are those who suffer from grave emotional and mental disorders, but many of them do recover if they have the capacity to be honest.

Our stories disclose in a general way what we were like, what happened, and what we are like now. If you have decided you want what we have, and are willing to go to any length to get it, then you are ready to take certain steps.

At some of these we balked. We thought we could find an easier, softer way. But we could not. With all the earnestness at our command, we beg of you to be fearless and thorough from the start. Some of us have tried to hold on to old ideas and the result was nil until we let go absolutely.

Remember that we deal with addictions–cunning, baffling and powerful. We also deal with all those memories of past hurts, misbehaviors and vows violated. Without help, our anger, hurt and mistrust are too great for us. But there is one who has all power; that one is God. May you find God now.

Half measures availed us nothing. We stood at the turning point. We asked God's protection and care with complete abandon.

1. We admitted we were powerless over our relationship and that our life together had become unmanageable.

2. We came to believe that a power greater than ourselves could restore us to commitment and intimacy.

3. We made a decision to turn our wills and our life together over to the care of God as we understood God.

4. We made a searching and fearless moral inventory of our relationship together as a couple.

5. We admitted to God, to each other and to another couple the exact nature of our wrongs.

6. We were entirely ready to have God remove all these defects of character, communication and caring.

7. We humbly asked God to remove our shortcomings.

8. We made a list of all persons we had harmed, and became willing to make amends to them all.

9. We made direct amends to such people wherever possible, except when to do so would injure them or others.

10. We continued to take a personal inventory, and when we were wrong, promptly admitted it to our partner and to others we had harmed.

11. We sought through our common prayer and meditation to improve our conscious contact with God as we understood God, praying only for knowledge of God's will for us and the power to carry that out.

12. Having had a spiritual awakening as the result of these Steps, we tried to carry this message to other couples and to practice these principles in all aspects of our lives, our relationship and our families.

Used with permission of Recovering Couples Anonymous.

PART II

Chapter 4: *Step One*

STEP ONE: We admitted we were powerless over our relationship and that our life together had become unmanageable.

Step One requires the admission of our inability to stop living in the extremes in our relationship. With no balance, we are like a light switch–either on or off.

A healthy relationship requires a rheostat–a mechanism that allows us a degree of middle ground. This need for a disciplined balance that relies on self-limits and boundaries is most evident in the two core issues we all deal with–intimacy and dependency.

The most obvious extreme is dependency on a mood-altering drug or experience (like eating, gambling or sex) in order to cope with life. The chemical or experience becomes the only source of nurturing that we trust, the primary focus of life for which everything else is sacrificed or compromised. This out-of-control style of living–what some call powerlessness–makes life unmanageable and chaotic.

For every out-of-control experience, there is an opposite extreme that is grounded in attempts at over-control. Many non-drinkers, for example, are as obsessed in a negative way with alcohol as are alcoholics. Some alcoholics binge and then abstain for days or weeks. Some bulimics both binge (overeat) and purge (vomit after eating). Couples may move, in the space of just a few minutes, from an emotional, abusive fight to making love. We know of only one way people can counter living in such extremes–they must admit that they could not and cannot control their behavior in spite of its negative consequences.

To accomplish this task, we need to look at another issue–intimacy. Those with problems, dysfunctional behaviors and/or addictions in their relationships (as well as those who support or enable them–the co-addicts or codependents) are missing and desperately seeking closeness, nurturing and love. In many ways, negative behaviors and addictions gain their compelling force because of a failure of intimacy. Addictive and obsessive behaviors are a futile, ineffective and ultimately destructive substitute for true caring and intimacy.

Without an emotional rheostat, people live an isolated, lonely existence in which they build walls around themselves, deny their needs, and share nothing of themselves. Conversely, they may find themselves so overly involved with one or more people that they feel trapped and smothered. They concentrate on meeting the needs of others (perhaps a partner) and take responsibility for their behavior. Boundaries do not exist; consequently, privacy does not exist. Again, a pattern of living in extremes emerges.

With the tools outlined in this book, it is possible to overcome the powerlessness and unmanageability in your life and relationship. The first step to do that is Step One. As part of Step One, you assemble evidence to document both the powerlessness and unmanageability you've experienced. This is the beginning of understanding the story of your dysfunction or addiction.

Remember, when we speak of "powerlessness," we mean being unable to stop doing a particular action in spite of its unwanted and negative consequences. When we speak of "unmanageability," we are referring to the chaos and damage created by the negative and/or addictive behaviors in your relationship.

"When we surrender, we stop struggling with the angels."

Shelly N., Al-Anon member

Step One is perhaps the most intense step you work as a couple. This step reminds you, and perhaps intensifies, the feelings of despair and hopelessness you've had about your relationship. The nature of Step One is to admit and experience the powerlessness you've felt over your relationship difficulties, and to admit that your life together has become unmanageable as a result.

The good news of Step One is that as you begin to admit and accept the powerlessness, unmanageability and despair you've experienced, the process of healing begins. The paradox of this step is that with surrender comes healing.

Remember, too, that we want this to be a gentle process for you. Take all the time you need to work through Step One. Seek out support for yourselves as a couple. Remember that no degree of difficulty you have experienced is unique to you. There are many other couples who have experienced similar feelings of powerlessness. You are by no means alone.

We suggest the use of separate paper if you need more space or privacy.

No. 1: First Meeting

Individual As a warm-up exercise for this Step, we ask you to sit down and remember your first meeting. When did the two of you first see each other or meet each other? Where were you? How old were you? Write your answers below.

Our first meeting was (place, time, etc.):

_____

_____

_____

_____

We were _____ and _____ years old.

We met under the following circumstances:

_____

_____

_____

_____

No. 2: Attraction

Individual After you mutually agree on the details of your first meeting, individually reflect on what first attracted you to your partner. Was it physical? Sexual? Emotional? Be specific. Was it your partner's gentleness? Personality? Charisma? Was there an intellectual attraction? If so, in what way?

The following are ways I remember being attracted initially to my partner:

_____

_____

_____

_____

_____

_____

_____

Now that you have completed the above exercises, we'd like you to compare your responses with your partner. Can you get in touch once again with the feelings of attraction, awe and wonder you felt in those beginning moments of your relationship?

Allow yourself to feel the warmth of those feelings. We believe that even though you may have found one another for some unhealthy reasons, the fact remains that you also found one another for some exciting and healthy ones, too. We encourage you to accept and try to re-experience those feelings now.

Genograms

Each of us has a unique family background, one with a long and rich history. As you begin your journey together, it is helpful to see your own and each other's families. These epic stories that we first discussed in Chapter One form the foundation that you bring into a relationship, and understanding them helps you see how you found each other.

As you move through this workbook, it is important for you to have a visual diagram of your family–a genogram, or symbolic way of representing your family on paper.

Below is an example of a genogram. We also list some symbols you can use as you create your genogram, but feel free to incorporate your own, too.

Some examples of genogram symbols:

◯	=	women	⊗ ⊠	=	death	**FA** =	Food Addict
▢	=	men	⊬⊬	=	divorce	**R** =	Rage
—	=	marriage	**A** =	Alcoholic		**Co** =	Co-dependent
⎸	=	children	**SA** =	Sex Addict		**DA** =	Drug Addict

Jason and Denell's family genogram

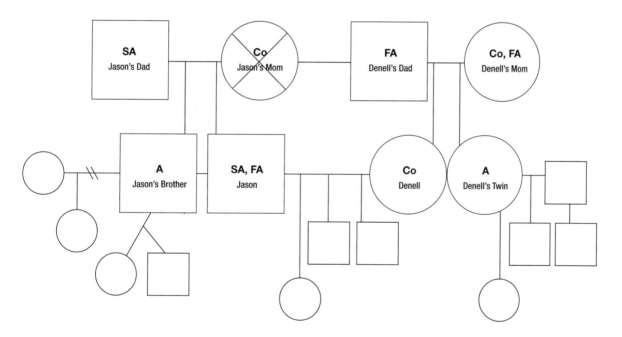

No. 3: My Family Genogram

Individual Create a genogram of your family in the space on this page.

Blending of Epics Worksheets

Each partner brings a family history to the relationship, an epic complete with heroes and horrors, victories and villains. Unquestionably, each partner's family affects the current relationship. To begin improving your relationship, it is essential first to see the unhealthy and dysfunctional patterns and/or addictions in your own families.

You have been on your own epic journey as a couple, drawing upon these earlier histories. It is important for each of you to identify the roots of powerlessness in your own history.

You may find that much of the trouble in your life today has existed in your family for generations. It has been passed down from parent to child to grandchild. You need to understand your epics so that you can break this pattern and learn healthy ways of relating—not only for the sake of your relationship, but also for your children's relationships, too.

At the end of each exercise, share your worksheet with your partner. You may not add to your partner's list, but you may ask her to clarify any areas you don't fully understand.

No. 4: Blending Our Epics

Individual As we discussed in Part One, every family, whether healthy or not, has set up its own boundaries. In this exercise, we would like each of you individually to list boundaries that you remember learning and experiencing in your family when your were growing up.

List boundaries which were too loose or too rigid, and ones which were appropriate and healthy. Identify the person or persons, both family and non-family members, who set the boundaries for you. Describe the impact these boundaries had on you.

Before you work on this exercise, you may want to refer to the discussion about loose and rigid boundaries in Part One, pages 21 and 22. Also feel free to consult other books on boundaries.

List as many or as few as you can remember. You don't have to list exactly five in each–you may have more or fewer examples.

LOOSE BOUNDARIES:	WHO TAUGHT ME:	THE IMPACT ON ME WAS:
Example 1: My parents invited me to their parties.	My parents	I felt like I had to grow up too fast. I felt I had to act like an adult when I was still only a child.
Example 2: My mother confided in me about things I shouldn't have been told.	My mother	I felt I was responsible for taking care of my mother emotionally, and later I felt like I was being used by her.
1. _____ _____ _____	_____	_____ _____ _____
2. _____ _____ _____	_____	_____ _____ _____
3. _____ _____ _____	_____	_____ _____ _____
4. _____ _____ _____	_____	_____ _____ _____

5. _____   _____   _____

_____   _____

_____   _____

RIGID BOUNDARIES:	WHO DID IT:	THE IMPACT ON ME WAS:
Example: I couldn't date Lutheran girls.	My parents	I was afraid to make mistakes; I grew up with religious prejudices.

1. _____   _____   _____

_____   _____

_____   _____

2. _____   _____   _____

_____   _____

_____   _____

3. _____   _____   _____

_____   _____

_____   _____

4. _____   _____   _____

  _____   _____

  _____   _____

5. _____   _____   _____

  _____   _____

  _____   _____

No. 5: Family Rules

Individual Think about the unwritten and unspoken rules in your family. Before you work on this exercise, refer again, if you like, to the discussion in Part One, pages 23-25, about the family rules of Don't Talk, Don't Feel, Denial, Minimizing and Blaming.

In the areas below, list examples of the ways you learned your family's rules. Identify the person or persons who taught you (both family and non-family members). Describe the impact these rules had on you. List as many or as few as you can remember.

DON'T TALK:	WHO TAUGHT IT:	THE IMPACT ON ME WAS:
Example: When I talked about not liking school, I was always told that I should like school.	Dad	I had (and still have) a hard time knowing what I don't like.
1. _____ _____ _____	_____	_____ _____

2. _____

_____

_____

3. _____

_____

_____

4. _____

_____

_____

5. _____

_____

_____

DON'T FEEL:	WHO TAUGHT IT:	THE IMPACT ON ME WAS:
Example: When my dog died, and I was sad, I was told, "Don't be sad, we'll get you another one."	My mom	I had a hard time feeling sad.
1. _____ _____ _____	_____	_____ _____ _____
2. _____ _____ _____	_____	_____ _____ _____
3. _____ _____ _____	_____	_____ _____ _____
4. _____ _____ _____	_____	_____ _____ _____
5. _____ _____ _____	_____	_____ _____ _____

TAUGHT TO DENY:	WHO TAUGHT IT:	THE IMPACT ON ME WAS:
Example: My parents didn't believe I could misbehave in school.	Mom and Dad	I learned to deny wrong behavior because I thought no one would believe I'd done anything wrong.
1. _____ _____ _____	_____	_____ _____ _____
2. _____ _____ _____	_____	_____ _____ _____
3. _____ _____ _____	_____	_____ _____ _____
4. _____ _____ _____	_____	_____ _____ _____
5. _____ _____ _____	_____	_____ _____ _____

TAUGHT TO MINIMIZE:	WHO TAUGHT IT:	THE IMPACT ON ME WAS:
Example 1: When my family had a problem, someone would say, "There's a silver lining in this cloud."	My parents	I never took my problems seriously. I thought they'd just get better with time and didn't try to do anything about them. This is still a problem
1. _____ _____ _____	_____	_____ _____ _____
2. _____ _____ _____	_____	_____ _____ _____
3. _____ _____ _____	_____	_____ _____ _____
4. _____ _____ _____	_____	_____ _____ _____
5. _____ _____ _____	_____	_____ _____ _____

TAUGHT TO BLAME:	WHO TAUGHT IT:	THE IMPACT ON ME WAS:
Example: Learned to blame my bad grades on bad teachers.	Dad	It's still hard for me to accept responsibility for my own performance.

1. _____   _____   _____

_____   _____

_____   _____

2. _____   _____   _____

_____   _____

_____   _____

3. _____   _____   _____

_____   _____

_____   _____

4. _____   _____   _____

_____   _____

_____   _____

5. _____   _____   _____

_____   _____

_____   _____

No. 6: Family Roles

Individual Before starting this exercise, refer to your family genogram and to the discussion about family roles in Part One, pages 25 and 26. Think about which members of your family played which roles. List the roles as well as who played them. Remember that different people can play the same roles, and that most people play a combination of roles. It is an unusual family that doesn't have each role being played by at least one person.

ROLES: **WHO PLAYED THEM:**

Hero: _____

_____

_____

Scapegoat: _____

_____

_____

Mascot: _____

_____

_____

Lost Child: _____

_____

_____

Enabler:

_____

_____

_____

Doer:

_____

_____

_____

Little Prince or Princess:

_____

_____

_____

Saint:

_____

_____

_____

No. 7: Stress and Tension

Individual In Part One, the ways in which families cope with stress and tension were discussed. In this exercise, we'd like you to list the unhealthy or addictive behaviors that you know existed in your family.

You may have grown up in what we call a perpetual family stress management seminar. If you did, there were times when you were shown or taught behaviors to bring down an excited, angry or anxious mood or bring up a depressed, sad or lonely mood. You were taught to alter your mood depending on the tension level in your family. There are members in your family who acted as a kind of barometer by sensing when emotions had risen or descended beyond a "safe" level, and then acted out to relieve the mood's building pressures and bring the situation back to "normal." By normal we mean what was normal for your family; this behavior should not be considered normal in a healthy family environment. Identify the individuals in your family who modeled these behaviors and/or addictions.

Additionally, in every family, there are some members who were aware of and tolerated these behaviors and/or addictions despite disliking them. They themselves were not addicted, but because they tolerate addictive or dysfunctional behaviors, we call them co-addicts. If you have difficulty identifying these individuals and their behaviors, then list the ways in which your family dealt with tension.

ADDICTIVE OR DYSFUNCTIONAL BEHAVIORS:	THOSE IN MY FAMILY WHO DID THESE BEHAVIORS:	THOSE IN MY FAMILY WHO TOLERATED THE BEHAVIORS (CO-ADDICTS):
Example 1: Alcoholism	My Father and Brother (Tom)	Mom, Grandma, Grandpa
Example 2: Frequent bursts of anger	Dad	Mom
1. _____ _____ _____	_____	_____ _____

2._____

_____

_____

3._____

_____

_____

4._____

_____

_____

5._____

_____

_____

No. 8: Abuse

Individual Most dysfunctional families have significant histories of emotional, physical, sexual and spiritual abuse, as noted previously in Part One, Chapter 3. The following worksheet helps you assess any abuse you experienced growing up. *Individually* list any types of abuse you remember experiencing. Also identify the person or persons who abused you (family or non-family member).

As you do this exercise, you may have painful memories about the abuse you experienced as a child. If so, try approaching it from a more detached viewpoint, like that of a reporter merely recording a series of events, rather than as one who has participated in them. Remind yourself that this exercise is designed to help you record your history so that you can better understand it.

Some of you may feel stuck when you delve into your past. You may have difficulty bringing back certain memories, or you may not be able to remember enduring any forms of abuse at all and that's okay. You can always add to this and subsequent lists as more information comes to you.

Some of you may have problems admitting to yourself that some members of your family might have wounded you. Many of us are charter members of what we call the Parent Protection League. PPL members are still trying to earn their parents' approval and have a strong need to come from a "healthy" family. PPL members often have an arduous time coming to grips with abuse experienced in their family. This, too, is fine for right now. If you feel stuck at any point in this exercise, leave it blank and move on.

Before you begin, you may want to refer to the discussion about abuse in Part One, pages 21-23.

> Many of us are charter members of what we call the Parent Protection League.

TYPE OF ABUSE:	THE ABUSER(S):	THE IMPACT ON ME WAS:
Example 1: I was told I was worthless and wouldn't amount to anything	Father	No matter what I accomplished, it never seemed good enough.
Example 2: Yelling, screaming and the use of profanities.	Both parents	Whenever anyone raised their voice, I panicked.
Example 3: Was never taught about sexual development.	Parents	Feelings of sexual awkwardness and shame, and an inability to have a healthy sexual relationship affect me even today.
Example 4: Was beaten and injured, and then didn't receive medical treatment.	My dad	I learned not to take care of myself. I learned to tolerate inappropriately high levels of physical and emotional pain.
Example 5: Was told that Jesus didn't like kids who did what I was doing.	Grade school teachers	Feelings of spiritual shame and guilt I have yet to shake off.
1. _____ _____ _____	_____	_____ _____
2. _____ _____ _____	_____	_____ _____

3. _____   _____   _____

_____   _____

_____   _____

4. _____   _____   _____

_____   _____

_____   _____

5. _____   _____   _____

_____   _____

_____   _____

At this point, offer your individual worksheets to your partner. This involves giving a special gift: a new awareness of yourself.

Receive each worksheet with the knowledge that it may have taken a lot of courage for your partner to give it. Each worksheet is a piece of your partner, a gift of honesty. It reflects an intent to become more intimate with you, both at this moment and in the future.

Compare your epic stories. Discover and discuss what you have in common and areas that were different for you in your respective upbringing.

You may find it helpful at this point to return to your family genogram and connect the behaviors you experienced and listed in the above exercises with the person(s) who modeled them for you.

For example, attach roles to those in your family who played them, note who taught you the various rules you learned, and mark those who had addictive behaviors.

This graphic representation helps you see how unhealthy and dysfunctional ways of dealing with others were transmitted between generations. It can also give both you and your partner a better understanding of your family background.

As you take part in sharing this information, you are not expected to solve the hurt your partner still holds, pain that stems from family-of-origin struggles. Nor do we expect you to provide all the nurturing needed to heal this pain.

The purpose of learning more about each other's epic story is to help you better understand one another, and to foster increased empathy and compassion for each other.

Now that you have completed this part of Step One, you can recognize the forces working against you as you tried to build healthy and intimate relationships in your adult lives.

Gentleness Break

You have just completed a significant piece of work. Congratulations!

Before you continue with more Step One exercises, stop and reward yourself. We encourage you to take a gentleness break at this time, and do something that is recreational and fun with one another. (If, at this point in your relationship, you have difficulty having fun together, then we suggest that you take this gentleness break individually.)

Choose one of the following activities as a way of being gentle with yourselves. If none of them appeals to you, find one of your own liking. If you feel compelled to keep on working, be aware that you can become compulsive about this workbook, too. Allow yourself to refresh and renew after the difficult work you've just successfully accomplished. So...

Pet a puppy.

Play with a child.

Enjoy a long nap.

Make a cup of tea.

Walk with friends.

Ask for a hug.

Do something frivolous.

Sit by a lake or a stream.

Work in a garden.

Meditate.

Listen to your favorite music.

Talk with a friend.

Read a novel.

Watch the sun set... or rise... or both!

Now that you feel refreshed and renewed, let's examine the impact your individual epics have had on your relationship. As you do so, you will have a new and deeper awareness of the influences that your families of origin had on your search for a partner. The various boundaries, roles, rules and dysfunctions/addictions that your family taught you–along with any abuse you suffered–had a profound impact on your search for a partner, as well as on how you have related to one another.

After completing each of the following exercises, share your worksheet with your partner. You may ask for clarification on any areas you don't fully understand. Feel free to ask for more examples. However, you may not add to your partner's list.

As you compare lists with your partner, you will undoubtedly feel some of the anger, pain and frustration you perhaps have felt many times before in your relationship. Accept these feelings. It's perfectly normal to have them. But also know that you don't have to resolve them now. If you feel the need to leave this work and get away from it for a while, take a Gentleness Break.

Step One Worksheet

Individual Acceptance of Step One paves the way to recovery. As you grow to understand your powerlessness in your relationship, and how unmanageable your relationship became when you tried to control everything about it, you will begin to understand the power that dysfunction and addiction have had over your life. "Unmanageability" means that your dysfunctional or addictive behaviors created chaos and damage in your life.

Some of you using this workbook may be unfamiliar with any of the 12-step recovery programs for addiction and their related terminology. Some of you may have difficulty accepting our use of the words "powerless" and "unmanageable" to describe relationships, or accepting that a person can be powerless over a relationship or an addiction. The words refer to a sense of a person's repeatedly frustrated attempts to improve a relationship.

To heal your feelings of powerlessness and unmanageability as a couple, each of you must first recognize how your own individual dysfunctions affected your relationship. This includes having a clear sense of how you were overwhelmed by the dysfunction of your relationship and how you coped in unhealthy ways, as well as accepting responsibility for the problems and dysfunctions that you personally brought to the relationship. This realization and admission help prepare you to use the rest of the Twelve Steps.

Completing the following exercises helps each of you to clarify your unhealthy behaviors in the relationship and their impact.

No. 9: List the ways you feel you violated boundaries in your relationship

BOUNDARY VIOLATION:

Examples:
Yelled and screamed at my partner.

At the end of the day when my partner needed to talk, I wouldn't.

1. _____

_____

_____

IMPACT IT HAD ON THE RELATIONSHIP:

My partner seems afraid of me.

My partner feels abandoned by me.

_____

_____

_____

2. _____   _____

_____   _____

_____   _____

3. _____   _____

_____   _____

_____   _____

4. _____   _____

_____   _____

_____   _____

5. _____   _____

_____   _____

_____   _____

No. 10: List ways in your relationship in which you have practiced your family's rules *(Don't Talk, Don't Feel, Denial, Minimizing and Blaming)*

Individual   The following examples show how the rules can be played out within the context of one relationship issue–family finances. In doing this exercise, you may wish to pick one issue in your relationship and explore it in the same way. You may also pick several issues and give examples for each of them.

RULE:	EXAMPLE OF USING THIS RULE:	HOW IT AFFECTED THE RELATIONSHIP:
Examples:		
Don't talk	I refuse to talk to my partner about any of our financial matters.	Since we don't talk about our budget, we're always in debt.
Don't feel	I often tell my partner not to worry about money because I'm taking care of it.	Not acknowledging and rejecting my partner's worries about money just increased her worries.
Deny	I always tell my partner that we have enough money even when the checking account is dry.	My partner spent beyond our ability to pay because he never knew how much money we had. It just made matters even worse.
Minimize	I often tell my partner, "Things are a bit tight now, but don't worry, I'll get a raise soon."	Minimizing the problem kept us from ever developing a strategy to get us out of debt.
Blame	I tell my partner to go get a better job if she wants more money.	Blaming my partner just made her feel worse about the problem and ashamed about our situation.
1. _____	_____ _____ _____	_____ _____ _____

2._____

3._____

4._____

5._____

No. 11: List the roles you think you play in your current relationship Individual

MY ROLE IS:	EXAMPLE OF HOW I'VE PLAYED IT:	IMPACT THIS HAS HAD ON THE RELATIONSHIP:
Examples:		
The Hero	I buy the cars, manage the checkbook and earn most of the income.	The responsibility creates a lot of stress for me, and resentment in my partner because she doesn't have any power.
The Enabler	I've totally managed the care of our children since their birth while my partner was working day and night.	I resent the inequity of this situation, and the children feel abandoned by my partner.
1. _____	_____	_____
	_____	_____
	_____	_____
2. _____	_____	_____
	_____	_____
	_____	_____
3. _____	_____	_____
	_____	_____
	_____	_____

4. _____

5. _____

6. _____

7. _____

8. _____

No. 12: List any dysfunctional behaviors or addictions you have or from which you are currently recovering

Individual Those of you who have no addictions do not need to do this exercise. Some of you may recognize and accept that you do in fact have an addiction from which you are not in recovery. If you have questions about whether this is true, or if you accept that it is true, please contact a 12-step organization for further help. See Resources on page 203 for more information.

It is difficult to do this workbook if you are just beginning to recover from a primary addiction. In that case, temporarily place your work here on hold. Once you have achieved a minimum of 30 days' sobriety from your addiction, then return to this workbook.

The goal of this exercise is to identify unwanted behaviors in your relationship which you haven't been able to eliminate, and to identify how these behaviors affected your relationship.

DYSFUNCTIONAL BEHAVIORS OR ADDICTION:	EXAMPLE OF POWERLESSNESS OR UNMANAGEABILITY:	IMPACT OF THIS BEHAVIOR ON YOUR RELATIONSHIP:
Examples: Financial Management	We have three different checking accounts, all of which are messed up; we are deeply in debt on credit cards.	We are always in debt, which causes a lot of stress for all of us.
Yelling at my kids	I can't seem to stop, in spite of all my efforts.	Kids are acting out in school, causing us stress; kids are afraid of me.
Alcoholism	I once spent my whole paycheck on a drinking binge.	Severe financial stress; embarrassment because my partner had to go to friends to get money to pay our bills.
Can't talk about my feelings with partner	Didn't tell my partner about my impending layoff at work until it happened.	My partner was furious and trusts me even less. Doesn't think I care about him/her.
1._____	_____ _____ _____	_____ _____ _____

2. _____

3. _____

4. _____

5. _____

Take a Gentleness Break

The work you have been doing is difficult. It takes honesty, courage and perseverance. Give yourself credit and a reward for what it has taken to work through the previous exercises. Do something nice for yourself.

Couple's First Step Inventory

When you compare your partner's worksheets with your own and begin to understand both families of origin and how they affect each of you individually, you are ready to talk to each other about the nature of the powerlessness in your relationship.

Couples taking a First Step together are surrendering to the powerlessness they feel over their relationship. They accept their feelings of having little or no control over the relationship–and its powerlessness and unmanageability. If you need to, review your individual First Step worksheets and use them as resources for completing the following inventory.

A gentle note: Completing any of the following sections may remind you of familiar, intense feelings of powerlessness, shame or despair. If this happens, get support from your sponsors. This is just the first step in a 12-step process. There is hope. Don't hesitate to take a break to find support for yourself.

Another suggestion: As you begin working through these exercises, you may find yourselves once again in old, familiar patterns of fighting, arguing and other dysfunctional behaviors that you have been caught up in for years. This is part of your powerlessness over your relationship. If this occurs, take a break from the process. If you cannot seem to avoid getting into these "historical" conflicts as you work these exercises, then set up a meeting with your sponsors to work these exercises in their presence.

The following inventory has eight sections. Each asks you to list five examples. There is no right number of examples. You may have three or 30. If you cannot complete a category, feel free to move on and return to the unfinished ones when you feel ready. When you complete all eight items, you will have a master list of examples of how your relationship has suffered because of powerlessness and unmanageability.

No. 13: List five effects that your individual dysfunctional/addictive behaviors have had on your relationship   *Together*

Examples:

Alcoholism led to a significant loss of money.

Denial of problems led to a point where we no longer had any idea how to solve them.

1. _____

_____

2. _____

_____

3. _____

_____

4. _____

_____

5. _____

_____

No. 14: List five unresolved major issues or problems in your life that do not go away no matter how hard you try   *Together*

Examples:
We can never seem to agree on who and how to manage our finances.

[One partner] just won't stop smoking.

1. _____

_____

2. _____

_____

3. _____

_____

4. _____

_____

5. _____

_____

No. 15: List five patterns in your relationship that you have tried to change which you have been unsuccessful at changing *Together*

Examples:

We never go to bed at the same time. We can't seem to talk without fighting.
We can't seem to find enough time to be alone together.

1. _____

_____

2. _____

_____

3. _____

_____

4. _____

_____

5. _____

_____

No. 16: List five lifestyle patterns you want to change but which persist   *Together*

Examples:

I'm always the breadwinner and my wife is always expected to stay home.

The wife is always responsible for arranging for babysitters.

The husband is always expected to take care of finances.

I go to bed at 10 p.m.; my partner never goes to bed before 1 a.m.

1. _____

_____

2. _____

_____

3. _____

_____

4. _____

_____

5. _____

_____

No. 17: List five ways you've "tried harder" together with no change `Together`

Examples:

We tried going out on dates.

We went to see a counselor, but it didn't seem to help.

We spent time with a financial counselor but still can't deal with our finances.

We went on a vacation at the suggestion of a counselor, but when we got back, everything was still the same.

Because we were having trouble communicating with one another, we tried to set up times to talk, but it didn't help.

1. _____

_____

2. _____

_____

3. _____

_____

4. _____

_____

5. _____

_____

No. 18: List five losses your relationship has experienced   *Together*

Examples:

Moving from Chicago to NYC.

Losing a lot of money because of an addiction.

Adultery in the relationship caused a loss of trust in one another.

Loss of friendships because we fight so much in public.

1. _____

_____

2. _____

_____

3. _____

_____

4. _____

_____

5. _____

_____

No. 19: List five ongoing sources of stress in your relationship that you've been unable to change

Together

Examples:
Chronic illness
Financial problems
Children
Jobs
Living situation

1. _____

_____

2. _____

_____

3. _____

_____

4. _____

_____

5. _____

_____

No. 20: List five stressful events in your life together over which you had no control   *Together*

Examples:
Death of a loved one
Laid off from a job
Illness of a child
Financial loss
Unwanted pregnancy

1. _____

_____

2. _____

_____

3. _____

_____

4. _____

_____

5. _____

_____

As you finish this couple worksheet together, you may experience a profound level of coupleshame. You may feel that you are the worst couple in the world, and that your relationship suffers from losses, stress and unmanageable difficulties that will never go away.

If this is so, you are not alone. You are experiencing the hopelessness and despair that many, many couples before you have also felt. It is time to tell yourself that there is much hope, and the first sign of that hope is your newfound ability to recognize these difficulties, talk about them and accept that they are problems in your life.

One thing to remember about despair is that it brings you to a point of brokenness and surrender in your relationship. This means you have come to a point where you recognize that you might actually give up on your relationship–that divorce is a very real possibility.

Interpret this act of surrender as a feeling that you have nothing to lose by becoming honest with each other. Doing so helps you combat the core belief we discussed in Part One which says, "If my partner really knew me, he/she would leave me." You're at that point anyway, so surrendering to your despair can lead you to the honesty you need to achieve intimacy.

Believe us when we say that your problems are not unique; they are experienced by many couples. Over time this process has enabled countless couples to recover.

Give yourself credit again for the fact that many of the problems you have experienced as a couple were based on relationship models you learned in your family of origin as a child. You've done the best that you could. You've survived. You're not yet divorced. And equally important, you're working through this workbook, an indication of how much you still care about each other and about preserving your relationship.

Also know that the intensity of your feelings of anger, despair and loneliness are indicators of how much you cared for one another at one time, if not still today. If you had never cared about your partner, you would not be experiencing such intense feelings at the thought of losing one another.

Although everything may seem hopeless, remember, this is called Step One because it is just the first step on the road to a better, more fulfilling, intimate relationship. There are 11 more to go. While you may be tempted to quit right now, hang in there. This stage is part of the *process*, and the *process* works. Trust in it.

Those of you who are working individual recovery program for an addiction will recognize that Step One, in all of its despair, was in fact the first step on the road to lasting sobriety. The feelings that you have now as a couple are the first step on the road to deeper intimacy and greater commitment.

> Surrendering to your despair can lead to the honesty you need to achieve intimacy.

Sharing your First Step

The final segment of Step One is to share what you have discovered about yourselves with at least one other couple. Many couples tell us that Step One becomes even more powerful when it is shared with another couple who can identify with and share their circumstance.

This Step invites you to share freely, holding little back. It means fundamentally acknowledging your struggles and surrendering to a different life. When you share this Step, focus on expressing the depth and pain of your struggles, not on telling the whole story. Choose incidents that are most moving to you. The goal is to see your situation even more clearly. The more honest you are, the more relief you will feel.

Taking this Step means openly admitting the patterns of your problems, and sharing the feelings that accompany the realization that you have been unable to control certain parts of your life together.

Healing occurs only when Step One goes beyond intellectual acceptance to emotional surrender.

We often use the words "powerless" and "unmanageable" when describing our relationship. But the paradox of recovery is that by admitting your powerlessness, you actually take the first step toward empowering yourself.

You have many talents and skills which you regularly and successfully use in your life. In your relationship, however, you have struggled because of the lack of tools and skills. This leads us to the purpose of this workbook: to develop and hone the skills needed to have the kind of relationship you have always wanted. The process now begins to move you toward greater commitment and intimacy.

Don't get stuck in your intellectual and rational self. Try instead to identify with the feelings of being powerless—feelings you have likely had many times as you tried to work on your relationship. Maybe you would prefer the word "stuck."

By using this workbook, you are empowering yourself to heal your relationship. It is one of the paradoxes of Step One that as soon as you admit powerlessness, you begin to get your power back.

The intensity of your

feelings of anger,

despair and

loneliness are

indicators of how

much you care for

one another.

Chapter 5: *Steps Two and Three*

STEP TWO: We came to believe that a power greater than ourselves could restore us to commitment and intimacy.

STEP THREE: We made a decision to turn our wills and our life together over to the care of God as we understood God.

Step One asks us to recognize and admit that we're having significant trouble in our relationship. Steps Two and Three ask us to confront the question of what gives our life meaning. Without meaning in our life, our relationship difficulties and struggles worsen. Without meaning in our life, we cannot establish the priorities which will help restore the balance, focus and self-responsibility we seek.

This question of meaning is ultimately a spiritual one. Steps Two and Three ask, In whom or what do you trust and have faith? Do you have spiritual beliefs? Do you believe that God, Allah, Jehovah or some Higher Power plays a role in your life?

A spiritual life is an essential ingredient in every couple's journey to reach greater levels of commitment and intimacy. As we grow in intimacy, our journey together into greater spirituality becomes a more significant part of our lives.

Many spiritual traditions speak of lifetime commitments by two people to each other. It is difficult to make such a commitment without the presence of a spiritual ground–a sense of what gives your life its ultimate meaning.

We have found that the extent to which people are able to trust a Higher Power and the extent to which they can trust the people in their lives, especially a partner, are often parallel. People who have no overriding sense of spiritual direction and meaning in their lives are unlikely to find trust and meaning in their personal relationships.

As it was originally written by Bill W. for Alcoholics Anonymous, this Step was devoid of any specific language about God. Bill W. did this because so many alcoholics who had come to AA had been judged or punished by various religious

> The extent to which people trust a Higher Power and the extent to which they trust the people in their lives are often parallel.

groups. Because of the anguish these experiences brought, many of these people were so turned off by religious language that a non-specific phrase had to be used for the word "God" to avoid triggering this pain. Although the AA standard and use of the term "Higher Power" are followed in this workbook, you are welcome to substitute the most comfortable wording for you.

We do not advocate any particular religious tradition. We recognize that couples using this workbook are from many religious backgrounds or no faith background at all.

Some of you have difficulty and conflict in your relationship because you came from different religious backgrounds. Carol and Steve were a couple who came from different sects of the same religion. Steve's sect firmly believed that they followed the "one path" to spiritual salvation. Since Steve's parents felt it was important for him to marry a woman from this same sect, they were never able to accept this relationship and withdrew from their lives.

Because of Steve's need to please his parents, he felt some guilt about having married the "wrong" woman, even though he deeply loved Carol. Disagreements over which church to attend were a continual problem in the marriage. Eventually, the two divorced. It was then that Steve's mother began speaking to him again, telling him that she was pleased with the divorce and that now he could finally seek the woman whom God had intended for him.

Carol and Steve's story illustrates just how much effect religious traditions can have on a couple's relationship. Try not to diminish or underestimate the power of your religious upbringing. It's important to understand each other's religious traditions (and the messages you still carry today from your upbringing) if you are to have a healthy relationship.

No. 21: Heritages

Individual This first exercise is designed to help each of you better understand your religious heritages. Write down in the space below the denomination(s) or religious group(s) you have participated in as a child and as an adult.

_____

_____

_____

When and for how long were you connected with or interested in each religion or faith?

_____

_____

_____

No. 22: Significant Religious Memories

Individual List memories of events in your life that hold religious significance for you, such as a particularly moving religious service, involvement in a church youth group, a confirmation or bar mitzvah.

_____

_____

_____

_____

No. 23: Spiritual Guidance and Authority

Individual List individuals in your life who have represented spiritual authority to you or provided spiritual guidance. Look beyond people who have traditional religious roles. Your choices may include people in your life who were very spiritual, yet did not have an official connection with a religion or hold any role of religious authority. They may be people who nurtured you and gave you guidance and support. Examples include close friends or relatives, a pastor, a nun or priest, a rabbi or parents.

_____

_____

_____

_____

No. 24: Significant Religious or Spiritual Passages

Individual List any passages from your religious or spiritual tradition that hold significant and deep spiritual meaning for you. For example, you might quote from the Koran, the Bible, the Bhagavad Gita or Lao Tsu's *Tao Te Ching*.

_____

_____

_____

_____

No. 25: Significant Religious Leaders

Individual List any significant religious leaders, heroes or other personalities (past or present) whom you hold in high esteem and from whose words and actions you draw inspiration and guidance, such as Gandhi, Martin Luther King, Jr., Jesus, Mohammed or Mother Teresa.

_____

_____

_____

_____

No. 26: Spiritual Music and Connectedness

Individual List any music you find to be spiritually uplifting or which brings you to a sense of spiritual connectedness or oneness. Examples could be "Amazing Grace," Beethoven's Ninth Symphony or Navajo drumming.

_____

_____

_____

_____

No. 27: Spiritual Places

Individual List places you visited which fostered feelings of awe and wonder. Perhaps it was a religious service you attended, walking the shore of the ocean, looking out into the star-filled sky on a clear winter evening, hiking in the mountains, a visit to an old and beautiful church, sitting at the side of a dying relative or friend or a quiet moment watching the sun rise over a still lake.

_____

_____

_____

_____

No. 28: Spiritual Teachings

Individual List any spiritual teachings you experienced in your past that you feel were negative or hurtful to you in some way. The numerous examples provided in this exercise are to help you get in touch with events in your life that harmed your spiritual growth.

Any experience of emotional, physical or sexual abuse at the hands of someone whom you viewed as a religious authority is, by definition, spiritual abuse. You may want to review the lists you made in Step One and take notice whether any of those who caused you harm were religious authorities.

DYSFUNCTIONAL BEHAVIORS:	THOSE IN MY FAMILY WHO DID THESE BEHAVIORS:	THE EFFECT THESE BEHAVIORS HAD ON ME:
Examples:		
I was told that if I continued to misbehave, I would burn in hell.	Father	I believed God hated me because I just couldn't be good all the time.
Never had any form of religious instruction.	Parents	I still have no idea how to make spirituality part of my life.
I was told that anger was unacceptable "in the eyes of God."	Pastor	I have great difficulty being angry, and when I am, I feel guilty about it.
I was told that all other religious groups were wrong.	Parents, pastor	I still have a hard time accepting other religious groups.
I was taught that no matter what I was experiencing, many others were much worse off.	Parents and other religious teachers	I just accepted my problems as my fate in life and I should not complain.
I was told that if I would only have enough faith, my problems would always get better.	Parents, pastor, friends	I began to think life was kind of magical: If I just prayed, read the Bible and went to church enough, all my problems would solve themselves and I wouldn't have to deal with them.

1. _____

_____

_____

2. _____

_____

_____

3. _____

_____

_____

4. _____

_____

_____

5. _____

_____

_____

Some of you may have difficulty thinking of examples for this or previous exercises in this Step. That's okay. It doesn't mean that you're not a spiritual person, or that you haven't had spiritual experiences. It may only reflect that your experiences may not have had as significant an impact on you as similar experiences have had on your partner or on others. It may mean that you don't yet recognize certain past experiences as spiritual. Or perhaps at many times in your past, you felt so overwhelmed with just trying to survive–to make it from one day to the next–that you were too tired or preoccupied to notice these feelings.

There's no shame involved here. These lists are simply designed to help you be in touch again with that spiritual part of yourself that we are working with now.

After completing the previous exercises, you most likely will have a greater sense of the spiritual "epic" you carry in your life and bring to your relationship. These experiences vary greatly. Some of you may have been force-fed religion, some may have had relatively healthy and positive religious experiences, and still others may have had no experience whatsoever. You now have a clearer idea of what you were taught as a child about God, how that view has changed (if it has) over the years and who helped shape those views.

Share Our Stories

Together   Now schedule a time together to take a walk, go out for coffee or in some way share each other's spiritual epic in a relaxed and private setting.

No. 29 Our Shield

Together In the second part of this Step, you are to create and draw a shield containing symbols representing how you as a couple see your Higher Power. Find some large sheets of paper to work on, and redraw the shield as you see it below using crayons, markers or colored pencils. A larger shield will make drawing easier.

Some of you will be muttering, "There's no way we can do this, we're not artists, we can't draw anything." You are not drawing for a teacher or an art contest, or anyone except yourselves. In fact, like many couples who have done this exercise, you may find that it becomes more fun (and even funny) as you go along.

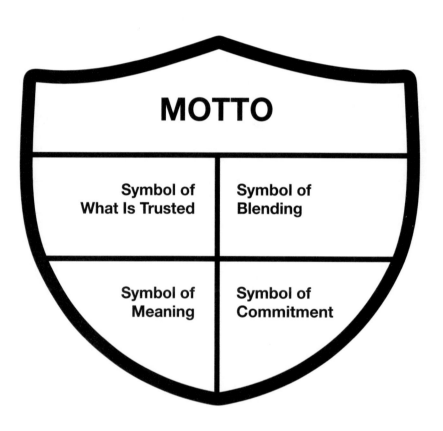

Your shield: Motto

In the section labeled "Motto" at the top of the shield, write a *meaningful phrase* that symbolizes your level of commitment to your relationship at this time. It may be a verse from a scripture or hymn, the title or phrase from a song that is important to you, or a phrase or sentence that you as a couple write.

At this point, some of you may not have much hope. That's okay. Let your motto and your shield reflect your present feelings, not what you want them to be or what you think they ought to be. One couple who attended a We Came to Believe weekend had such feelings, and chose this title from a Rolling Stones song: "You Can't Always Get What You Want."

Your shield: Quadrant 1–Spiritual sources

In the upper right-hand corner, draw symbols representing the *spiritual blending* in your lives. In Step One, we talked about the blending of the family epics from which you came. In this quadrant, symbolize the part of that blending which you see as spiritual. Depict the spiritual strengths that you each bring to the relationship.

For example, one of you may have come from a deeply religious family background and still finds that this gives you strength. One such person we know drew a Bible to represent this. Another couple drew a picture of their family sitting around the dinner table and saying a prayer. Still another couple drew a pulpit because both their parents were pastors. There are an infinite number of ways you can represent this idea. Whatever symbols you choose are fine so long as they hold meaning for you *as a couple*.

Some of you may be unable to draw anything in this quadrant because you don't feel either of you brings any spiritual strengths to the relationship. If so, it is okay to leave this quadrant blank for now.

Your shield: Quadrant 2–In whom we trust

In this upper left-hand corner, draw symbols that represent what you *trust* together as a couple. If what you trust is God or a Higher Power, you may have trouble depicting this. If so, you will be helped by the story of the mother who found her 8-year-old son at his desk drawing a picture of God. She said to him, "But nobody knows what God looks like." He replied, "Well, they will when *I* get done!"

You may also choose symbols of religious authority or institutions. Some of you may choose to depict people or institutions you've come to trust that are not necessarily thought of as religious, such as politicians, teachers, a trusted friend or a counselor. There are no right or wrong symbols.

Your shield: Quadrant 3–Meaningful mementos

In the lower left-hand corner, draw symbols of things or people that are *meaningful* to you. What have been the most meaningful things in your life as a couple? What have you put your energy into creating or acquiring?

Your symbols might depict secular or religious leaders, institutions or groups. If you have been or are a member of a 12-step recovery group or other support group, you may choose to depict this. Some couples have drawn a symbol for money, for example, because they recognized and admitted to themselves that their highest goal in life actually had been the pursuit of money and possessions. Other couples have drawn symbols for status or power or athletics or children. Be rigorously honest with yourselves as you ask yourselves this question. If your symbol is unrelated to spirituality, that's okay. The purpose of this exercise is to help you see yourselves *as you are now*–not how you want to be.

Your shield: Quadrant 4–Commitment

In the lower right-hand corner, draw symbols for your *commitment* to one another *as it is today*. Some couples in the We Came to Believe weekends drew two interlocking rings, and others drew two people standing in front of an altar in a church. We have seen couples draw music notes which symbolized a song that they felt reflected their commitment. A house or children may be a symbol of your commitment because it's been your children who have kept you together. Another couple drew a question mark in this quadrant because they weren't ready to decide what level of commitment they had to one another.

Wrapping up

Step Two contains the phrase "We came to believe." It implies the *process* of coming to believe. In completing Steps One and Two, you accepted that you didn't have the power and knowledge on your own to create the kind of relationship you wanted. That feeling of despair can be the starting point in coming to believe that only a Higher Power can help you attain what you desire.

There are many ways to conceive of a Higher Power. Some people view this as a supreme being, called Allah or God. Others do not. Many people who are recovering from an addiction feel that their Higher Power is the friendships they found in their recovery groups. It was only through these friendships, and the support and accountability they provide, that these people could attain sobriety. To them, this is a Higher Power.

By working through this Step, you are in the process of coming to an understanding of what you believe to be a Higher Power.

STEP THREE: We made a decision to turn our wills and our life together over to the care of God as we understood God.

In Step Two you became more aware of the beliefs you share as a couple about God or your Higher Power, and the conflicting beliefs with which you struggle. The Third Step phrase, "We made a decision to turn our wills and our life together over to the care of a Higher Power" means that you are willing to accept the help of a Higher Power–something greater and beyond yourselves.

Coming to this point of acceptance happens for some people during a dramatic moment. For others, it develops slowly, evolving over time. The process of accepting is not as important as your ultimate commitment to make spirituality part of your daily life together. Also it is not important that you both agree on a theological doctrine or a specific definition of a Higher Power. It's about creating a spiritual life together, embarking on a spiritual journey.

Some couples feel that both partners have made a personal decision to turn their life over to a Higher Power. For other couples, only one partner may have come to this decision. This situation can be a source of great conflict, particularly if the partner who made such a spiritual commitment believes that his decision is the correct one. Sometimes such individuals are unwilling to live with a partner who has not made a spiritual commitment. For other couples, neither partner has made any commitment to bringing spirituality into their life. Regardless of your position, continue together on your spiritual journey.

After completing Step Two, you have a better idea of the religious strengths you bring to your relationship and what you both find meaningful. To prepare for the tasks of Step Three, work through the following exercises.

As part of developing an identity, we all experience different phases of dependency (how much we depend on others for help). These phases can be defined as follows:

Dependence–we need and want help.

Counterdependence–we need help but resist it.

Independence–we are self-sufficient and do not need help.

Interdependence–we both give and receive help.

No. 30: Identity *Individual*

When you can't find something in a grocery store, do you (check one):

____ Keep searching until you find it?

____ Ask for help?

When putting something together from a kit, do you (check one):

____ Follow directions carefully?

____ Quickly go through the instructions only when you get stuck?

____ Figure it out yourself?

When you are personally in pain and need support, do you usually (check one):

____ Talk to people immediately?

____ Wait until the crisis is over and then tell people?

____ Get through it the best you can without help?

As you responded to these situations, did you discover a pattern of not accepting help? People in dysfunctional or troubled relationships tend to rely primarily on themselves.

No. 31: Dependency

Individual You may have learned not to depend on people for help, care or support. This approach is probably based on the way your primary caregivers treated you as a child. Consider the following list of people. How did they affect your ability to accept help? Did they support you when you made a mistake? Did they show you how to do things, or did they expect you to know how to on your own?

Your father:

_____

Your mother:

_____

Brothers and sisters:

_____

Other significant adults (specify):

_____

Teachers (specify):

_____

Employers (specify):

_____

Clergy (specify):

_____

No. 32: Perceptions of a Higher Power

Individual For most of us, perceptions of a Higher Power evolve over the years. Before you can be truly reflective about a Higher Power, it is important to clarify your attitudes. The following exercise is designed to help you do this.

The view of God most people hold falls into these four categories:

A punishing God who punishes our mistakes but does not reward or help.

An accepting God who accepts that we fail and cares anyway.

A non-involved God who is detached and unconcerned with our lives.

A nonexistent God from whom no help is available.

These ways of seeing God can interfere with attempts to determine your relationship with a Higher Power. How do you view the role of God or a Higher Power in your life?

_____

_____

_____

_____

_____

_____

No. 33: Attitudes Toward God   **Individual**

Name the five persons who most influenced your attitudes toward God or a Higher Power.

1. _____

2. _____

3. _____

4. _____

5. _____

Do they have anything in common?

_____

_____

_____

_____

No. 34: Higher Power Working in Your Life

Individual To explore in greater depth the experience of the Higher Power working in your life together, ask yourselves this question: In what ways do you see a Higher Power working in your life right now?

1. _____

2. _____

3. _____

4. _____

5. _____

No. 35: What Does "Turning It Over" Mean?

Individual The challenge of Step Three is to arrive at some agreement about what your daily spiritual journey will be like, particularly as you seek to invite a Higher Power into your lives over the coming days, weeks and months.

If you were to turn your lives together over to the care of a Higher Power, how would you go about doing this? Based on what you have learned thus far, what will turning it over mean to you now?

_____

_____

_____

_____

No. 36: Obstacles and Strengths of Your Religious Background **Individual**

What obstacles does your religious background or upbringing create for you in trusting a Higher Power?

_____

_____

_____

_____

What strengths does your religious background or upbringing create for you in trusting a Higher Power?

_____

_____

_____

_____

What other obstacles might prevent you from accepting the help of a Higher Power?

_____

_____

_____

_____

The process of turning it over in Step Three is not a one-time event; but rather a daily journey. Think about what this process could be like for you as a couple. The task of Step Three is to arrive at some agreement about what this spiritual journey is like for you.

Write a Spiritual Journey Contract for the coming days, weeks and months, and share it with your sponsors. Keep in mind that there is no correct formula for these activities. You may develop a variety of approaches and exercises on your own. With spiritual journeys, there are many paths to the same truth.

Here are examples of what other couples have done.

Read meditations each day together. Many choices are available to those who seek spiritually uplifting literature such as daily-meditation books, texts from religious organizations or books on spirituality. Read from one on a daily basis.

Daily prayer. Praying together and sharing each other's spirituality can be one of the most intimate activities two people can do together. If you have not been able to be intimate and vulnerable in other ways with each other, praying together may be difficult. If you want to try, realize that this is an activity that you may need to develop slowly. Some couples find that simply reading prayers others have written is a good way to begin.

Renew your vows. Some couples find that the initial step on their joint spiritual journey is to renew their original commitment to each other. For them, making such a lifetime commitment is part of what they hold to be ultimately meaningful. The commitment may be made by formally declaring a marriage vow, or by making a more personal statement to each other. It may be made in the presence of your sponsors, or with a person of spiritual or religious authority.

Physical journey. You may find that it is important to make a physical journey or pilgrimage to a place that holds spiritual significance for you. Some couples have even traveled to the Middle East to locations sacred to their religious heritages. Others have gone to places within the Unites States. One Native American couple traveled to the Black Hills of South Dakota because of its deep spiritual significance and power for them.

Time in natural settings. Some couples find that they want no part of anything that reminds them of institutional religion, whether it be meditation, prayer or a place of religious significance. Their spiritual journey may include simply taking walks together to enjoy the tranquility of nature. One couple from a workshop spent a week hiking in the mountains of Montana to experience the majesty of the Rockies.

Choosing a new religious group. It is not unusual for partners to find that they have experienced individually or mutually judgment or abuse at the hands of a particular religious group. Because their unhealthy or dysfunctional behaviors were classified by their religious tradition as wrong and sinful, they may have experienced judgment and exclusion. A return to either partner's traditions would be difficult.

Many of us have been wounded in this way by institutions which claim to be caring and humanitarian. This contradiction has created much confusion about spirituality–as well as a fair amount of anger–for many people. For now, any association you have with a religious institution may be only temporary. In spite of previous wounds from religious institutions, a time of reconciliation may be important at some point. In the future, your spiritual quest may bring you to make a more permanent commitment to a new group.

Whatever your situation, it is our belief that religious institutions ought to be caring and supportive, and a safe and comforting place. You may need to seek out a religious institution that doesn't remind you of past pain.

You may want to go "church shopping." Visit various churches, participate in their activities, and see if you can sense the presence of gentleness and caring. Does the institution encourage and support your relationship to your Higher Power?

A fellowship of couples

Some couples find that simply participating in a fellowship of couples provides the spiritual foundation they need for their journey. If there is a Recovering Couples Anonymous group in your area, consider visiting it to see if it can provide this spiritual link.

How you choose to make your journey is only your business. Don't compare your choices to those of others, and don't let your choices be judged by others.

No. 37: Spiritual Journey Contract   *Together*

Write down what your spiritual quest will be like. Ask your sponsors to sign this contract when you've completed it.

_____   _____
Signature of Partner   Signature of Partner

_____   _____
Signature of Sponsor   Signature of Sponsor

_____
Date

In closing…

Many people who grew up with unhealthy and dysfunctional behaviors in their families and who feel a sense of shame are often on a quest for approval. Often they seek black-and-white answers to their questions, including those about their spirituality. Believing that you belong to the "correct" religious group provides a kind of ultimate security. Such thinking also leads to rigid and provincial thinking and living. These attitudes are often experienced by others as judgment.

As partners, be gentle with one another, and recognize that the answers you may be tempted to push on your partner may be related to your own insecurities rather than to a connection with your inner truth and Higher Power.

Celebrating your progress

Congratulations on completing your first three Steps, which are so crucial to this process. These Steps can be difficult at times, and you may find yourself feeling sad or even ashamed. If so, seek the support of others who can reinforce the work you are doing.

A suggestion: Create a celebration for yourselves to mark your progress! What are some gentle, healthy ways you can celebrate the new beginning you are making? What are some of the ways you can celebrate your progress as you work through this book during the coming weeks and months?

Chapter 6: *Steps Four and Five*

STEP FOUR: We made a searching and fearless moral inventory of our relationship together as a couple.

STEP FIVE: We admitted to God, to each other and to another couple the exact nature of our wrongs.

In Step One, you admitted your inability to have the kind of relationship you want, and that your relationship and life had become unmanageable.

In Steps Two and Three, you learned how to gain the support you need from your Higher Power and other people to face the reality of the problems in your relationship. You also made a commitment to surrender control of your relationship to the help that is available from your Higher Power as you understand it.

With this support, you are ready to make a fearless moral inventory and use it to examine and repair the problems and damage you have brought to yourselves and others around you.

Such an assessment can impel you to let go of much of what keeps you in destructive and unhealthy patterns. This part of recovery requires that you give up the old ways in which you coped by living out of balance.

One of the first challenges of the Fourth Step is to ask, "How have I been wonderfully made?"

"Sometimes I define intimacy as 'into me see.' I have to look at myself first."

Nancy, Al-Anon member

This Step commonly brings up feelings of discomfort, anger, fear, shame, sadness and loneliness. The Fourth Step can be a deeply personal experience for each of you as you pass through layer after layer of feelings into a deeper relationship with yourself and each other. Steps Four and Five are designed to remedy the feeling of coupleshame. In telling your moral inventory to others in the Fifth Step, you discover that there are those who have had similar experiences to yours, and who are ready to forgive you and offer you their support.

The work of Step Four is to examine your relationship by taking a moral inventory of your life together in all its respects. As you begin this Step, keep in mind that no relationship is totally healthy and none is totally unhealthy.

This Step offers a way to reclaim the good parts of yourselves and use them to improve your relationship.

> *Some people bridle at the word "moral" in the Fourth Step. It's one of those vestigial terms from when the steps were originally written in the 1930s. Words like "moral" and "defects of character" in the Sixth Step were really referring to what is now called character development, the areas we need to improve. Semantics aside, the inventory focuses on the deeper, harder work on which the Twelve Steps are centered.*

Often people who are having difficulty in their relationship can't see the good that is there. If it is difficult for you to take credit for the positive parts of your relationship, perhaps you have grown used to working hard to cover your dark side, and to show only the good parts to the world. You may have lived in between the secrets, shame and abuse of the down side of your relationship and the care, responsibility and values of your "public" side. You probably feel phony about your relationship's public side, because people don't know the truth behind the image you showed the world. Perhaps you feel that the good stuff doesn't count because there is a side about which you feel embarrassed and ashamed.

A Fourth Step moral inventory of your relationship becomes your teacher by showing both your positive and negative sides. For example, ask yourself whether it took strength to maintain this life? Endurance? Cleverness? A willingness to risk? And resourcefulness? You possess all of these and more–qualities that are equally available to you for healthy uses as your relationship recovers and grows stronger.

By looking for both the good and the bad, this Step offers a way to reclaim the good parts of yourselves and use them to improve your relationship. You don't have to have a powerless, unmanageable side draining all your power in its secrecy, and you don't have to feel phony or insincere once you can embrace your whole selves. What's more, it is much easier to improve your relationship when you acknowledge the many positive traits you have to draw upon, as well as the strength available to you through your Higher Power.

The Fourth Step is a demanding and sometimes draining experience. Pace yourself. Take several gentleness breaks. It is difficult and important work, so take all the time you need.

Fourth Step Inventory

We begin this Step by asking you to do some individual work first. To prepare for your couple Fourth Step, both of you need to look at your individual strengths and weaknesses, and the impact that they have on your relationship.

One of the first challenges of the Fourth Step is to ask yourself the question: "How have I been wonderfully made?" All of us have numerous talents, skills and abilities. One of the ways to recognize yours is to ask yourself what do you do that gives you a sense of joy? What activities give you a deep, inner sense that you are doing what you're supposed to be doing (rather than what others want you to do)?

No. 38: Self-Affirmations

Individual Spend some time thinking about the many positive qualities you possess. In what ways are you enjoyable, loving, caring and trustworthy? Sometimes your positive traits may be more obvious to others than to yourselves. Ask a close friend for help.

Examples:

I have a great sense of humor.

I am a person with much courage.

1. I am/have _____

_____

2. I am/have _____

_____

3. I am/have _____

_____

4. I am/have _____

_____

5. I am/have _____

_____

In the following exercises, look at all aspects of your life and how they affect your relationship. In the left column, record things in your life that you view as needing improvement. In the right column, record your strengths.

Depending on the relative health of your relationship, your answers may be more on one side or the other in each category. If your relationship is still functional, your answers will tend to fall more to the right. If not, your answers will fall more to the left. Sometimes you may have nothing to place in a category. That's okay. When you finish these exercises, you will have a clearer view of your individual contribution to the strengths and weaknesses of your relationship.

Complete the following questions about your role in the relationship. You will be sharing these later with your partner.

No. 39: Using Talents, Skills and Abilities   *Individual*

In what ways have I not fully appreciated and used the talents and skills that I have?	In what ways have I fully appreciated and used my talents and skills and offered them to my partner?

No. 40: Self-Responsibility Individual

How have I failed to take responsibility for my actions and mistakes?

_____

_____

_____

_____

_____

How have I taken responsibility for my actions and mistakes?

_____

_____

_____

_____

_____

No. 41: Accuracy and Honesty Individual

In what ways have I placated my partner, practiced denial, minimized problems or my behavior, or avoided sharing my real perceptions?

_____

_____

_____

_____

_____

In what ways have I been honest with my partner?

_____

_____

_____

_____

_____

No. 42: Separateness/Connection *Individual*

In what ways have I developed a life separate from my partner, family and friends? In what ways have I not been available to my partner or provided the chance to connect regularly?

In what ways have I been available for my partner and actively sought ways to share my life, friends, activities and interests with him/her?

_____

_____

_____

_____

_____

_____

_____

_____

_____

_____

No. 43: Shame/Approval *Individual*

In what ways have I looked for things to go wrong in our relationship, and/or sought to blame my partner for them?

In what ways have I been able to give affirmation and approval to my partner in our relationship?

_____

_____

_____

_____

_____

_____

_____

_____

No. 44: Personal Needs Individual

In what ways have I not nurtured my own personal needs or expected my partner to intuitively know them, and been angry when she/he did not? When I was in emotional or physical pain, how did I fail to care for myself?

In what ways do I nurture myself? How have I been clear to my partner about what my needs are? In what ways did I care for myself appropriately when I was in emotional or physical pain?

_____

_____

_____

_____

_____

_____

_____

_____

No. 45: Clarity in Making Choices Individual

In what ways have I avoided making decisions by either leaving them undecided or by forcing my partner to make them? How have I been unclear about my likes and dislikes?

In what ways have I made healthy and prompt choices and decisions? How have I stated clearly my likes and dislikes?

_____

_____

_____

_____

_____

_____

_____

_____

No. 46: Stress *Individual*

In what ways have I allowed myself to become overextended to the point where I am overstressed and have little left to give emotionally, physically or spiritually to those in my life?

How do I seek relaxation and play, take time to keep the demands in my life in balance, and replenish myself physically, emotionally, mentally and spiritually?

_____

_____

_____

_____

_____

_____

_____

_____

No. 47: Sharing Feelings *Individual*

In what ways have I not shared uncomfortable feelings with my partner?

What uncomfortable feelings have I shared with my partner?

_____

_____

_____

_____

_____

_____

_____

_____

No. 48: Finishing Business `Individual`

How have I avoided resolving such issues as arguments, decisions and other major issues in our relationship?

How have I sought to work with my partner to resolve unfinished business in the relationship?

_____

_____

_____

_____

_____

No. 49: Parenting `Individual`

What have been my weaknesses as a parent?

What have been my strengths as a parent?

_____

_____

_____

_____

No. 50: Providing   *Individual*

In what ways have I avoided my responsibilities to provide financially, physically (e.g., home maintenance), emotionally and spiritually for my partner and family?

In what ways have I been a good provider for my partner and family?

_____

_____

_____

_____

_____

Couple's Fourth Step Inventory

Now that you have completed the Individual Fourth Step Inventory, you may want to review your answers and use them as a basis for the Couple Fourth Step Inventory.

Look at the following questions and answer those that apply to your relationship. Depending on the relative state of your relationship, you may have a number of answers in the negative categories. Remember to give yourselves credit for the positive responses, too. You may want to look at your answers in a few weeks or months and use them as a measure of the improvement in your relationship.

The primary goal of this inventory is to help you gain a better awareness about the relative health and dysfunction in your relationship.

No. 51: Giving/Parenting   *Together*

In what ways have we given so much outside the relationship that it was harmful to ourselves or others, such as giving so much to community activities, work or our children that we had nothing left to give each other?

In what ways has our giving to others been meaningful and satisfying, while maintaining a balance in our time and energy?

_____

_____

_____

_____

No. 52: Isolation/Community   *Together*

In what ways have we isolated from other couples and friends, cutting ourselves off from their support and community?

In what ways have we sought community for our relationship by seeking out other couples and friends?

_____

_____

_____

_____

No. 53: Crisis   *Together*

In what ways have we handled crises poorly–in our family, in our relationship and among friends? In what ways have we created a crisis by blowing a situation out of proportion?

In what ways have we dealt with crises well?

_____

_____

_____

_____

_____

No. 54: Conflict   *Together*

How have we dealt with conflict? Have we repeated fights over the same issue? Have we deliberately created conflict over relatively superficial issues to avoid a deeper issue?

How have we dealt with conflicts so that they were resolved and both of us were generally satisfied with the process and the result?

_____

_____

_____

_____

No. 55: Relationship *Together*

In what ways have we neglected our relationship in such areas as communications, recreation and spirituality?

How have we nurtured our relationship by taking time for each other and playing together?

_____

_____

_____

_____

_____

_____

_____

_____

No. 56: Stress *Together*

In what ways have we allowed ourselves to become so depleted of spiritual, physical and emotional energy that we have nothing left to give anyone?

What steps have we taken to manage stress so that we could maintain balance in our lives and ensure a continuous reservoir of energy with which to nurture ourselves and others?

_____

_____

_____

_____

_____

_____

_____

_____

No. 57: Intimacy   *Together*

In what ways have we avoided telling each other who we really are or what we really feel?

_____

_____

_____

_____

_____

In what ways have we been open, honest and trusting enough to reveal who we really are and what we really feel?

_____

_____

_____

_____

_____

No. 58: Our Identity as a Couple   *Together*

In what ways have we felt that we were so bad as a couple (coupleshame) that no one would accept us or want to be with us?

_____

_____

_____

_____

_____

In what ways have we felt confident in ourselves as a couple, been able to acknowledge both our strengths and weaknesses, and enjoyed our time together and with others?

_____

_____

_____

_____

_____

No. 59: Denial/Acceptance　Together

What are the issues in our relationship that we pretend don't exist and have avoided dealing with?

What are the issues we have acknowledged, faced and talked about?

_____

_____

_____

_____

_____

_____

_____

_____

No. 60: Boundaries　Together

In what ways have we practiced setting poor boundaries in our relationship and thus tolerated abuse in the relationship and in our families? Have we, for example, allowed our parents to wound our children in the same ways they wounded us?

In what ways have we set appropriate boundaries and protected ourselves and our family members?

_____

_____

_____

_____

_____

_____

_____

_____

No. 61: Spirituality   *Together*

In what ways did we avoid bringing spirituality into our relationship?	In what ways have we been spiritual together as a couple?
_____	_____
_____	_____
_____	_____
_____	_____
_____	_____

Step Five: Sharing your inventory

STEP FIVE: We admitted to God, to each other and to another couple the exact nature of our wrongs.

When you complete your Couple Fourth Step Inventory, you have a deeper awareness of the strengths and weaknesses of your relationship. There are things you can feel joyful about, and others that you may feel appropriately sad and guilty about. Remember, guilt is not shame. Guilt is honest remorse for mistakes that you have made.

The remedy for appropriate guilt is to share your Fourth Step with another person or couple. This helps you see yourselves as the partners you are. A successful Fifth Step comes from sharing your written inventory with another person or couple who will recognize and note your sources of deepest feeling and the problems you've been unable to solve. They can remind you that you are not the first couple to make mistakes, nor will you be the last. The loneliness of the Fourth Step now becomes an opportunity to reach out. A special connection occurs when someone accepts you even though they know the very worst things about you.

With whom would it be most meaningful for you to share your Fourth Step? Whom would you most want to hear the moral inventory you have just finished? It may be your sponsors, or you may choose a person of religious/spiritual authority. Think carefully before making this choice.

Once you have made a decision about whom you will tell, contact them, explain to them what you would like to do, and arrange at least an hour's time to go over your Fourth Step Inventory.

The whole Fifth Step does not have to be completed in one sitting. Some people who regularly listen to Fifth Steps recommend it be done in two or three sittings rather than in one marathon session.

Many couples have told us that completing the Fifth Step was a turning point in their relationship. It gave the first three Steps new meaning, and they felt for the first time that they were really a part of the process.

The two of you and the person or couple with whom you share your Fifth Step may want to record your reactions and feelings about the progress you have made in the space below.

_____

_____

_____

_____

_____

_____

_____

_____

_____

_____

_____

> Many couples say that completing the Fifth Step was a turning point in their relationship.

Take a Celebration Break

Your relationship is still alive and you are putting in great effort to improve it through *Open Hearts*. After the difficult work of these first five Steps, do something to celebrate your togetherness.

Go out to dinner.

See a play or movie.

Walk in the park.

Go to an amusement park.

Go roller skating.

Chapter 7: *Steps Six and Seven*

STEP SIX: We were entirely ready to have God remove all of these defects of character, communication and caring.

STEP SEVEN: We humbly asked God to remove our shortcomings.

In earlier Steps, particularly Steps Four and Five, you learned about some of your shortcomings. Many of these were learned originally as defenses or coping mechanisms to survive a difficult childhood. For example, isolating yourself might have been the only way you could find to cope with abuse in your family.

Now that you have chosen to work to improve your life and your relationship, you can release these unhealthy and ineffective ways of caring for yourself and learn how to replace them with healthy ones.

Step Six follows naturally from the previous five Steps, which have helped you identify many of the problems or "defects" in your relationship. You have completed a moral inventory of your relationship, and you've shared it with each other and another person or couple of your choosing.

Now you can begin working for improvement in your relationship by incorporating tools that will help you remove its defects. Steps Six and Seven build from Steps Two and Three, and the realization that only your acceptance of a Higher Power working in your life will help you effectively make these changes.

Begin your work on these next two Steps by recalling the work you did in Step One. If it has been a while since you last looked at Step One, review those exercises now. Don't be alarmed if looking back on your Step One work brings up a feeling of despair; it is through feelings of weakness that strength begins to grow.

A word of caution: While you have been working hard and have moved quite far in this process, there is a problem that can stop your progress, what many people call "relapse" or a slide backward into old habits and ways. Within you are "friends" of your old ways: pride, willfulness, jealousy, grandiosity, depression and suicidal

"I'm in charge of the action; Higher Power is in charge of the results."

DICK, AN AL-ANON MEMBER

preoccupations. These are aspects of yourself which make you vulnerable to relapse. They are shortcomings which can return you to the compulsive and unhealthy ruts you were in before you began this process. Some of these shortcomings may have helped you survive in the past, but now they are a gateway to disaster. One of the purposes of the exercises in Steps Six and Seven is to help you avert relapse.

"I'm outta here"

It is important to recognize first that one key defect in your relationship is how you have managed conflicts between the two of you. As Part One discussed, few couples are given the tools to recognize, express and deal with conflict.

In the development of relationships, couples get to the point when the honeymoon is over and they begin to recognize problems in each other–the Separation Stage. Few couples have the ability to deal effectively with the conflicts that are commonly found in this relationship stage.

When conflicts arise, as they inevitably do in all relationships, partners who never learned to deal with conflict when they were growing up will deal with the problem by "exiting," threatening to leave or abandoning the relationship.

Exits are any means taken to avoid dealing with the conflict partners experience in the relationship. Exit behaviors include physically leaving for a time (hours, days or even weeks,) working late, going out with friends, agreeing to work on community committees to keep away from your partner and over-involvement with children. Other exit behaviors are more classically addictive, such as drinking too much, endless TV watching, compulsive spending, gambling or shopping.

Note that some people also move into particular emotions to avoid conflict. Raging so as to frighten one's partner and children away from any communication is also an exiting behavior. Others may assume a "poor, helpless me" act that impels the partner to feel sorry for him or her and thus suspend dealing with whatever conflict has arisen. Others may simply seek refuge in alcohol or other drugs, or withdraw into themselves.

In this exercise, list the ways you have exited your relationship by using alcohol or other drug(s). Substance exits can also include excessive use of food, caffeine or nicotine.

No. 62A: Substances   **Individual**

List any substances you use or have used to lower or raise your moods and thus help you avoid dealing with conflict.

_____

_____

_____

_____

No. 62B: Behaviors   **Individual**

List other behaviors you have used to avoid dealing with conflict in your relationship.

_____

_____

_____

_____

Now that you have each completed Exercise No. 62, Parts A & B, come together and compare your respective lists.
- Were you aware of how you were exiting the relationship to avoid problems?
- Were you aware of your partner's exiting behaviors?
- Ask your partner if he or she was aware of your exiting behaviors.
- If so, ask what effect your behavior had on them.
- Perhaps at this point you will notice that the partner who did not exit the relationship when a particular conflict arose became frustrated when the other "left." This can sometimes intensify the feelings of conflict.

If tools for conflict resolution are not used, the effect will be to drive the partners into ever deeper resentment of each other.

No. 62C: Exiting   *Together*

Combine your lists of the ways the two of you exit the relationship. In the first column, write how partner A exits the relationship. In the next column, write how partner B reacts when he/she notices this behavior is happening.

Exit Behavior	Partner's Reaction

Digging deeper

Every couple has a set of unhealthy behaviors they use to deal with conflict, especially at times of high stress or personal emotional exhaustion. Sometimes these behaviors occur when there would otherwise be an opportunity for emotional intimacy, but one or both partners avoid closeness by initiating these behaviors. It is crucial to recognize these patterns and the temporary insanity they bring into the relationship.

The chart on pages 132 and 133 helps organize your thinking about ways you have mutually lost touch with reality.

Here are some examples of dysfunctional patterns with which couples avoid intimacy in their relationship.

Repetitive arguments

Arguing repeatedly but never resolving the same issue(s) persists because it gives partners a screen to avoid dealing with underlying issues.

For example, one couple argued for years about balancing their checkbook. Nearly every month when their bank statements came in the mail, they would argue over who was at fault for the financial mess. This argument was a convenient way to avoid facing deeper issues of financial management in general and how the responsibility for the family finances should be divided. To discuss these issues required a level of relationship intimacy that both feared.

Keep in mind that a repetitive argument is not the same as a healthy, regular expression of conflict or the expression of a true difference of opinion on family budgeting.

Frequent periods of denial

A couple may indeed have trouble in their relationship but refuse to admit it. One couple, for example, experienced sexual dysfunction. They had difficulty being intimate with each other in other ways in their relationship, and this lead to an infrequent and dissatisfying sex life. Although this was particularly frustrating to one partner, this partner would deny the problem and insist that "everything's fine" when pressed by the other. We know couples for whom such a problem grew so severe that they had no sexual relationship whatsoever. Yet, rather than talk about their problems, the partners just avoided sexual intimacy.

Nonproductive communications

Some couples talk about everything under the sun except the problems they face. On the surface, these couples may seem to communicate well because they talk a lot to each other. This is, however, an illusion. Numerous couples in our workshops could rattle on about the upkeep of their house, their jobs or their kids' school careers, but when it came to talking about their feelings for each other or their relationship problems, they suddenly became silent. For such couples, talk has become merely a tool for filling their lives with the shell of communication.

Extension and depletion

Some couples become emotionally depleted. Consciously or unconsciously, couples often pack their schedules so, exhausted, they have no time for each other, let alone for true intimacy.

A typical situation involved two partners who worked long and difficult hours. Besides work, the husband involved himself with the kids' activities, including coaching their sports teams. Then he was elected to a community board which required nearly 20 hours a week. His wife assumed all domestic responsibilities and volunteered for numerous church and community activities. This hyper involvement guaranteed little presence in each other's lives. During the few moments that arose for meaningful conversation, both partners were so exhausted that healthy, intimate communication was impossible.

Making statements you don't mean

Sometimes couples make statements that deflect attention from an issue at hand. Criticizing your partner or finding fault with your partner over a trivial matter are two ways to do this.

For example, a husband regularly criticized his wife about the care of the house. Her response was to belittle his ability to earn enough money, stating that if he earned more, she could hire a housekeeper and maintain it to his liking. This cyclical round of criticism distracted them from the issues that they were truly dissatisfied about in their relationship.

In other examples, partners make rash statements in the heat of non-productive arguments, statements that they really don't mean. Sentences that start with "You never ..." or "You always ..." usually introduce such statements.

Taking actions that you regret

In the heat of the moment, some couples take actions that they are ashamed of later. An example of this is a couple who never talked about their conflicts. Every few months, however, some event or statement would trigger the deep-seated anger that had built up. When the inevitable explosions occurred, one partner would shout and use profanity. The other would hit things or throw objects around the house. Once they had cooled down, both deeply regretted their behavior. Unfortunately, the effect of their actions was to frighten each other enough to discourage any productive discussion of the issues at hand. True intimacy was thus avoided.

The previous list of examples is by no means complete. There may be other patterns of craziness which you can identify in your own relationship. Often when couples look back on these patterns of craziness as third-party observers, the behaviors actually seem funny. As a way to begin changing your patterns, try to see the humor in the patterns you have used.

No. 63: How Do We Know When We Are Acting Crazy?   *Together*

We suggest that you begin Exercise No. 63 when you are both feeling rested and when you're not in the middle of a conflict. Go to a comfortable and safe place where you will not be distracted. Then, fill out the following chart.

In the left column (Pattern Description), describe your patterns, including the actions each of you take.

In the next column, partner one will list the feelings he/she has in response to the pattern. This could include anger, fear, sadness or loneliness, for example.

In the third column, partner two will list his/her feelings in response to the pattern.

Now notice if there are any similarities in the way you each feel during the pattern. For example, perhaps both of you feel afraid, even though the pattern you've described shows you acting angrily with one another. Or you both may be feeling lonely, while in the pattern you are both making critical statements to one another.

As you begin to notice similarities or differences in your feelings and qualities such as the frequency of the pattern, write what you have noticed about this pattern in the last column.

PATTERN DESCRIPTION:	1st PARTNER FEELS:
1. _____	_____
_____	_____
2. _____	_____
_____	_____
3. _____	_____
_____	_____
4. _____	_____
_____	_____
5. _____	_____
_____	_____
6. _____	_____
_____	_____
7. _____	_____
_____	_____
8. _____	_____
_____	_____

2nd PARTNER FEELS:

_____

_____

_____

_____

_____

_____

_____

_____

_____

_____

_____

_____

_____

COUPLE NOTICES:

_____

_____

_____

_____

_____

_____

_____

_____

_____

_____

_____

_____

_____

The goal of this exercise is to help each of you recognize the repetitive behaviors in your relationship, and the feelings that are involved when you are doing these behaviors.

We hope you see the discrepancies between your actions and feelings by doing this exercise. Perhaps you also notice how infrequently either of you communicate your real feelings and how much you really care about your partner.

Moving on

The first exercise gave you a picture of how each of you reacts in your relationship when you're not openly and honestly expressing and handling your true feelings. The second gave you a look at the defects of character, communication and caring in your relationship.

Next, in Step Seven, you will learn how to remove those defects.

Ten firestarters

The following ten issues can be deadly for couples. As you look over this list, circle or note those which trouble your relationship. Not all couples have problems with every one, but most find some troubling. You may also have difficulty with other issues not included here. Feel free to add them to this list.

- Sex

- Money

- Kids

- Roles

- Trust

- Past behaviors

- Controlling your partner's "mistakes"

- Partner's family

- Unfair fighting

- Separate interests

STEP SEVEN: We humbly asked God to remove our shortcomings.

Communicating with one's Higher Power is a most personal experience. For some of us, it involves praying, reading scriptures or going to religious services together. For others, it may mean consulting a spiritual mentor or meeting with other couples to discuss problems.

The best path for you is the one you know in your heart to be right for you. Review the work you did in Step Three. What does your act of surrender to your Higher Power in Step Three tell you about how to work this Step? As you take your spiritual journey seriously, you will want to seek the help of your Higher Power.

Opening our minds to a new approach

One technique that may help you move ahead is found in many spiritual traditions. It speaks to the need to become child-like before transformation can occur.

Because of the problems, dysfunction or abuse we experienced in our family of origin, many of us lost our ability to be childlike. To recover, you may need to rediscover and embrace that part of yourself that remembers how to be honest, playful, spontaneous and courageous.

This exercise is designed to help you contact that little child within you. The first part is done individually, but it is most effective if you do this exercise simultaneously, and then get together immediately to share your experiences.

Find a quiet, peaceful and comfortable place where you will not be disturbed by noise or other people. You may want to have some relaxing music or nature sounds playing in the background.

Once you have created these conditions for yourself, read through the following narration and allow yourself to experience the thoughts and feelings that come to you in this relaxed state. Stay with this state for as long as you like. When you're finished, take as much time as you need to write down what you discovered and felt.

If you prefer, another way to do this exercise would be to have a friend slowly read the following narration to you. You may also want to have this friend narrate this visualization onto an audiotape which you can then play back whenever you wish in your chosen place of peace and quiet.

However you choose to do this exercise is fine; what is important is that you choose a way to get in touch with your most reflective self. Many rational thinkers have some initial difficulty doing meditative exercises. Don't be discouraged if you do. You may need to repeat the exercise several times before you are able to gain insights, so stay with it. The very fact that this exercise is somewhat difficult for some of you may also indicate how early in your life you were deprived of your ability to be in touch with this part of yourself.

Some couples may have a healthy and appropriate parental reaction to the nurturing needs of their own little child or that of their partner. Allow yourselves to have this reaction and to talk about it with each other. You may discover that you do have the inner ability to nurture yourself and your partner. The reason you haven't done so in the past is not that you didn't have the skills, but that these skills somehow had been blocked.

Part of the work of Step Seven and of subsequent Steps is to unblock these skills. In many ways, the two of you are now becoming nurturing parents to the "child" that is your relationship together. As you both grow in awareness of each other's "little children" and the "child' that is your relationship, we encourage you to use your parental skills to nurture that relationship.

No. 64: Visualization

Allow yourself to relax. Imagine that the weight of your body is passing down from the top of your head through your neck, your shoulders, down through your arms, your torso and stomach, down through your legs until all of your weight is draining slowly out through your toes.

Your body is feeling more and more relaxed as more and more of your weight passes down and out your toes. You feel very light and comfortable without all that weight.

Notice that while this is happening, your breathing is becoming slower and more rhythmic. With every breath that you exhale, more tension leaves your body.

As you experience this wonderfully relaxed feeling, allow your mind to concentrate on this narration. Turn your attention to the sound of my voice. Begin a journey in your mind, imagining that you are standing by the shore of a lake, a lake whose waters are calm and incredibly blue. It's so peaceful there as the sun shines brightly. The air is warm, with a cool breeze flowing off the lake. You feel cool and refreshed, so relaxed, comfortable and safe as the sun gently warms you.

As you walk along, from the opposite direction coming toward you, you see a little child. As this little child gets closer and closer to you, you realize that this child is you when you were 3, 4 or 5 years old.

As this child comes up to you, and you know this child is you, you take the child's hand and the two of you begin to walk together by the lake.

As you do, the little child begins talking to you, hand in yours. You sense clearly that this child trusts you and will be honest with you. You ask this child how he or she is doing, and the child begins to tell you. As you walk together, you listen to all that the little child has to tell you.

[Pause]

You continue to walk and you hear all that your little child has to tell you—the secrets, the feelings, the experiences, the pain that your little child possesses.

Now imagine that as you are listening to this, you kneel down and you give a hug to your little child. You tell your little child how much you love him/her, and that you are there any time you little child wants to talk to you.

Then you stand up again and continue to walk. As you do, you see another little child coming toward you. As this little child gets closer, you realize that this is the little child of your partner at age 3, 4 or 5.

As this little child comes up to you, you take this child's hand, too, and the three of you begin walking together by the lake. Feel the warmth of the sun, the cool breeze, smell the blooming wildflowers. All around you is beauty and gentleness and love.

As you walk, you ask your partner's little child how she/he is feeling. Your partner's little child begins to tell you, and as you walk, you listen to all your partner's little child has to tell you.

———————————————— [Pause] ————————————————

Now imagine that as you are listening to this, you kneel down and you give a hug to your partner's little child. You tell your partner's little child that you hear and understand. You tell your partner's little child how much you love him/her, and that you are there any time he/she wants to talk to you. You are there as a friend.

Then you stand up and continue walking together. Eventually, when it feels right, you let go of both their hands. As you do, you see that they take one another's hand and run off into the distance, laughing and talking together, delighting in each other and all the beauty and tranquillity that surrounds them and you. You wave to them–these two little children, one that is you and the other that is your partner–and as you wave to them, you know that they will be back. They will be there to listen to you, too, whenever you want.

As you watch them, they move off in the distance. When you feel ready, you are invited to slowly come back to the place where you are sitting and slowly open your eyes.

———————————————— [Pause] ————————————————

Processing the visualization *Together*

Gently allow yourself in your mind to return to the place where you were in the visualization. If you feel comfortable, write down the thoughts and feelings that came to you while doing this exercise. Take as much time as you wish.

For some of you, this may have been an emotional exercise that brought feelings of sadness or even tears. If so, take a gentleness break together.

Next, both partners need to find a quiet and comfortable location where you can be together without being disturbed. Share with each other what you experienced and learned about yourselves in this exercise.

THIS IS WHAT I LEARNED ABOUT:

A. My little child

_____

_____

_____

B. My partner's little child

_____

_____

_____

Many couples who did this exercise during our workshops found it is sometimes difficult to be in touch with the deep emotions that can surface in this exercise. When you do this exercise, you may remember an experience or have feelings related to a childhood experience for the first time. If this happens to you, seek support from your sponsors, a close friend, clergy person or counselor to work through this experience.

You may also find that this is an exercise filled with emotion for you as a couple. Be gentle and understanding with each other and seek the support of another couple, counselor or others if you feel you need this.

Dependency Dimensions

The following chart looks at the healthy and unhealthy ways we need each other. The left side lists seven categories of healthy ways we need and depend on each other. The right side gives examples of unhealthy or dysfunctional dependency. The two sections are mirror images of one another.

In the "receptivity" category, for example, people who have healthy dependency seek the help of others, let others help them, trust others, and can admit and talk about their inadequacies. Healthy dependency means we can recognize our inadequacies, ask for help, and accept it. In the "receptivity" category under unhealthy dependency are people who resist help, hate feeling inadequate, ignore advice and distrust others.

The other six categories likewise show qualities of healthy and unhealthy dependency.

	HEALTHY DEPENDENCY	**UNHEALTHY DEPENDENCY**
Receptivity	I will seek help I can ask for advice I can feel "little" and be okay I trust the help of others I talk about anxiety and feelings of inadequacy	I resist assistance I hate feeling inadequate I ignore advice I distrust others' motives I never talk about my inadequacies
Reliability	I follow through on things My behavior and attitudes are predictable I finish tasks I perform agreed-upon roles, functions, and plans I have a history of keeping promises I continue dealing with a conflict until it's resolved	I'm unpredictable I break promises I look for ways to avoid or escape conflicts when they occur I leave much business unfinished
Responsibility	I admit my mistakes I take responsibility for my behavior I acknowledge problem areas I see my own limits I work to see my role in conflict I make amends when I've done harm to others	I blame others I disguise my misbehavior I cover up mistakes I avoid dealing with my problems I distort reality to avoid responsibility

	HEALTHY DEPENDENCY	UNHEALTHY DEPENDENCY
Autonomy	I am clear about boundaries I can operate independently I appreciate time alone I have a strong sense of self I can hold values contrary to others' opinions	I am anxious when alone I'm confused over boundaries I'm easily influenced by others I have a high need for approval I'm unsure about who I am
Assertiveness	I ask for wants/needs to be met I take action to make plans happen I don't let my life pass by I identify areas of conflict I'm willing to struggle with conflict	I avoid conflict I alienate others with demands I intimidate others I "sell out" in conflict I negotiate my own needs away (I won't fight for myself)
Respect	I regularly affirm myself I regularly affirm others I let others solve their problems I recognize the stage of development others are in I nurture self-esteem in others I see others as competent to handle all that life brings	I try to protect others from reality I make shaming statements I try to reform or change others I diminish myself and others I try to solve others' problems
Cooperation	I readily give assistance I share leadership I make suggestions I work with others to find new solutions to problems I collaborate on implementing plans	I seldom if ever help others I work on most things by myself I need to invent my own solutions I operate independently of others' efforts I agree on plans with others, but then I do what I want anyway

No. 65: Dependency Rating Scales   **Individual**

To do this exercise, find a quiet place where you can be alone. Look at the dependency rating scale below. The scale on the left is for rating yourself, and the one on the right is for rating your partner. (This is the first time in working an exercise where you take your partner's inventory as well as your own.)

To begin, look at the receptivity category in the Dependency Dimensions chart. If you feel that the descriptions of healthy dependency in that category fit you perfectly, give yourself a 10. If you feel that the unhealthy characteristics fit you perfectly, give yourself a 1.

On the other hand, if you are like most people with both healthy and unhealthy characteristics in this category, you fall somewhere in between 1 and 10 on the scale. Rate your partner on this Receptivity category in the same way. (Please note that you have only temporary permission to evaluate your partner.) Now fill out the rest of the categories as you did the first, rating both yourself and your partner on each.

When you both have completed this exercise, exchange your charts with each other. Remember this information is not for you to numerically rate either your partner or yourself. Many couples notice how much their ratings agree. Others notice that they rate themselves lower than their partners rate them. Whatever the case, this is an opportunity to discuss how you relate when it comes to dependency. The categories also give you ideas about qualities on which you may want to work in the future.

DEPENDENCY RATING SCALES

	YOU	PARTNER
	LOW HIGH 1 2 3 4 5 6 7 8 9 10	LOW HIGH 1 2 3 4 5 6 7 8 9 10
Receptivity	1 · · · · · · · · · · · · · · · · · 10	1 · · · · · · · · · · · · · · · · · 10
Reliability	1 · · · · · · · · · · · · · · · · · 10	1 · · · · · · · · · · · · · · · · · 10
Responsibility	1 · · · · · · · · · · · · · · · · · 10	1 · · · · · · · · · · · · · · · · · 10
Autonomy	1 · · · · · · · · · · · · · · · · · 10	1 · · · · · · · · · · · · · · · · · 10
Assertiveness	1 · · · · · · · · · · · · · · · · · 10	1 · · · · · · · · · · · · · · · · · 10
Respect	1 · · · · · · · · · · · · · · · · · 10	1 · · · · · · · · · · · · · · · · · 10
Cooperation	1 · · · · · · · · · · · · · · · · · 10	1 · · · · · · · · · · · · · · · · · 10

Intimacy Dimensions

Now that you have begun to understand healthy and unhealthy dependency, a similar exercise helps you look at your ability to be intimate.

On the chart the seven sections of the left column list qualities of healthy intimacy; the right states qualities of unhealthy intimacy. In the Initiative category, for example, healthy intimacy includes being able to reach out to others, risk expressions of caring (saying "I love you" or "I missed you"), invite others to share activities, share and talk about their problems with others, and express their desires and needs to another. Those who have problems with intimacy are passive and isolated, unable to ask for what they need, assume the role of victim (they feel they have little or no power), and often feel as though no one cares for them.

	HEALTHY INTIMACY	UNHEALTHY INTIMACY
Initiative	I will call on others I reach out to others I risk expression of caring I invite others to share activities I share problems/concerns	I'm passive I am able to express desire and attraction I'm isolated I act like a victim ("Things just happen to me; I have no control over my life")
Presence	I initiate activities I meet others I listen I pay attention to others and the world and life around me I have explicit reactions to people and events I'm open with my feelings I take part in activities with others regularly I notice details	My feelings are constricted I'm unavailable to others because of feelings of shame I deflect both positive and negative attention away from myself, believing I don't deserve either My obsessions block attention that might come my way
Closure	I finalize arrangements I acknowledge and care about others I acknowledge others who desire my time, or who are attracted to me I work to conclude things I express thanks	I make everything into a crisis I'm out of control; so overextended that loose ends are everywhere in my life I avoid closure I can't resolve problems or concerns

	HEALTHY INTIMACY	UNHEALTHY INTIMACY
Vulnerability	I share problems I share my process of thinking and feeling I reveal myself and share who I am with others I involve others in decisions I talk about myself	I keep my thoughts private My decision-making process is private My internal dialogues are secret and unshared, but I still rely on them
Nurturance	I make caring statements, and I care for others I'm empathetic I support others I make suggestions I help others in need I provide feedback to others I let other people know that they have value	I always try to take care of others I don't allow others to have feelings I discount or diminish others and/or their efforts
Honesty	I acknowledge my positive and negative feelings I'm clear about my priorities and values I am specific about disagreements	I don't acknowledge that I have deep feelings I seldom, if ever, express my preferences I disguise anger in order to have sex I rely on third parties to communicate with my partner
Play	I can see humor in life I put effort into leisure time I celebrate joyful events I'm willing to dance I explore new ventures with others I like to smell flowers I enjoy children I laugh easily	I'm compulsively busy I miss significant events I have a grim demeanor, a "life's a mess" attitude I don't experiment in life I'm compulsive about hobbies

No. 66: Intimacy Rating Scales *Individual*

As you look at the scales, notice that they are set up exactly like those in the Dependency Dimensions section. The scale on the left is for you, and the one on the right is for your partner.

To begin, look at the Initiative category in the Intimacy Dimensions chart. If you feel that the descriptions of healthy intimacy in that category fit you perfectly, give yourself a 10. If you feel that the unhealthy characteristics fit you perfectly, give yourself a 1. On the other hand, if you have both healthy and unhealthy characteristics in this category, you will fall somewhere in between 1 and 10 on the scale. Likewise, rate your partner on the Initiative category, also.

Now fill out the rest of the categories just as you have done this one, rating both you and your partner. When you finish, you will have a chart that shows an intimacy rating for both of you.

When you both have completed this exercise, exchange your charts with each other. Use this information to begin discussing the concept of intimacy with each other.

Again, pay attention to where and how much your ratings agree or disagree. Take this opportunity to discuss the relative state of intimacy in your relationship. The categories also give you ideas about qualities of healthy intimacy to work on in the future.

You may want to work on some of the dimensions of Intimacy or Dependency that are a problem for you. If you do, clarify which ones you're going to work on, and on how you address each issue. For example, perhaps you and your partner decided that in the intimacy category entitled "Play," you want to dance more.

First, ask yourselves what specific steps you need to take to make dance a greater part of your life. You might check in the phone book for places that teach dancing or look in the newspaper for clubs that have music you like. Your reticence to dance may stem from embarrassing childhood experiences about dancing. Or it may relate to a core belief that you are not able to dance well enough for your partner, and that she will leave you because of this. Share your feelings with your partner as you become aware of them. This is another way to be courageous in your relationship and to take risks.

For more help on working through such tasks as these, refer to the following sections on problem solving, fighting rules and fighting contracts.

INTIMACY RATING SCALES

	YOU	PARTNER
	LOW HIGH 1 2 3 4 5 6 7 8 9 10	LOW HIGH 1 2 3 4 5 6 7 8 9 10
Initiative	1 · 10	1 · 10
Presence	1 · 10	1 · 10
Closure	1 · 10	1 · 10
Vulnerability	1 · 10	1 · 10
Nurturance	1 · 10	1 · 10
Honesty	1 · 10	1 · 10
Play	1 · 10	1 · 10

Healthy fighting
Before you begin...

Do not do this exercise alone. Your sponsors can be of particular help to you in this exercise, and you may want to work through it with them, a counselor or a clergy person. Often couples slip into old patterns of fighting even as they are trying to develop rules and parameters for healthy conflict resolution (what we call "fair fighting").

Begin this section by first taking time individually away from your partner to list the actions or incidents that happen when you are fighting–actions or incidents that seem to you to be unhealthy, unfair, destructive or that make you feel afraid. These could be things that either you or your partner or both of you do.

Don't be confused by the use of the word "fighting." In this exercise you are to look at your perception of what it means to fight. To begin with, it doesn't mean a physical, knock down, shouting battle. Also, a fight does not have to be dramatic. A fight can be carried out merely be speaking directly, clearly and strongly to one another, perhaps occasionally with a moderately raised voice.

The following is a short and incomplete list of aggravations drawn from couples who have participated in our workshops.

- Blaming
- Using only "you" statements ("You did this," "You always do such and such")
- Swearing
- Trying to out-yell one another
- Hitting or threatening to hit
- Fighting in front of the children
- Throwing things
- Arguing in inappropriate places (in a restaurant, at the home of friends, in front of friends, in public)
- Name calling
- Case building (calling up everything you can think of from the past that supports your contention that your partner is wrong and stupid.)
- Button-pushing (deliberately mentioning sensitive areas you know will infuriate your partner)
- Temporarily exiting the relationship–either physically or emotionally

As you create your list, pay attention to your feelings. Are you afraid? If so, try to think of your fear as a friend telling you about the ways you have fought unfairly in your relationship.

Once you have completed your list individually, come back together in the presence of your sponsors and combine your lists. You now have a complete list of all the ways both of you have been expressing anger and frustration–ways that bring up feelings of fear and unfairness.

Developing fighting rules and contracts

In the next part of this exercise, create a fighting contract from your combined list, a list of rules that you mutually agree to abide by during all expressions of conflict. These rules should be agreed upon in front of your sponsors.

The main purpose of a fighting contract is to encourage you to recognize and deal with the conflicts that inevitably come up in any relationship. The difference is you do so in healthy, productive ways so you feel safe and can resolve the conflict.

Feeling safe means that you feel protected from emotional or physical battering. Fighting in safety, however, most likely will feel much safer than any fight you've ever been in before!

For many of you, any expression to your partner about disagreement, anger, resentment, dissatisfaction or other feelings can cause extreme anxiety if it's been your experience that your partner retaliated in some way. Having a fair fight may mean that you mutually agree not to emotionally or physically distance yourselves–no matter what is said. It may take quite a while and a lot of practice before you really feel safe expressing your feelings and having a fight. This is new territory. It's natural to feel afraid. One of your rules may be that you agree to have a fight even though one or both of you is afraid to do so.

As you begin these exercises, keep in mind that when you are able to tell your beloved just how angry you are, it is a gift to your partner. It shows you love him or her enough to be honest.

We suggest adding the following rules to your fighting contract:

> When you are able to tell your partner just how angry you are, it is a gift that shows you love him or her enough to be honest.

Agree on the fight

For a fight to take place, both of you first must agree that it is a fight.

How does this process work in day-to-day life?

As days pass, you may notice that some problem seems to worsen into a source of conflict between you. When this happens, an alarm should go off signaling you both to put your fighting rules into effect. You need to agree that this is indeed a conflict that you both need to talk about.

Agree on a time and place to fight

Setting a time and place to fight after agreeing to fight 1) allows time to cool down and collect your thoughts, and 2) prevents one partner from being ambushed by the other.

Your contract may include agreeing to agree to fight on a more regular basis. For those of you who have seldom fought, the concept of fighting regularly may be very strange. For example, you may decide that on every Sunday evening at 6:00

p.m., you will each agree to make a list of the things that have made you unhappy in your relationship in the past week–and then exchange lists. This will be your way of handling conflict. You may further agree to be honest about and list feelings of resentment, anger, loneliness.

Set time limits on your fights

Because fighting can produce a lot of anxiety, put a time limit on your fights. At first you may only be able to fight for a few minutes, so agree to limit it to 15 minutes.

Some of you may find yourselves fighting endlessly, even into the wee hours of the night. Try agreeing to fight for a limited time, 30 minutes perhaps, and then schedule a resumption of the fight the next day at a time on which you both agree. In order to resume fighting the next day, you may have to ignore previously held beliefs about not going to bed with a fight unresolved.

There are couples in which one partner is a marathon fighter, a situation which so frustrates the other partner that he temporarily leaves the relationship to get out of what seems to be a neverending conflict.

Set a time limit with which you both feel comfortable. That means you both agree to stay there physically and be there emotionally for the duration of the fight. While you may call for a time-out and take a break, no exiting is allowed.

Sometimes couples find that during a time-out they both are able to relax a little and collect their thoughts, and then come back to finish the fight with a clearer idea of their feelings and desires.

The value of setting limits is that, no matter what limits you set, you have the safety of knowing that no fight is really out of control.

Fighting in the presence of a third party

As you begin to make changes in your relationship, you may find that you just don't yet have the skills or the strength to abide by your contract on your own. You may want to add the additional rule that you agree only to fight in the presence of your sponsors or another person. If this is the case, don't be discouraged. You are like countless other couples who, with time and practice, eventually became able to fight in a healthy way on their own. Like any other skill, this one also takes practice to achieve mastery.

Fighting in front of children

Another question we are often asked is whether fights should ever take place in front of children. The easiest and initial answer to this question is no, if the style of fighting will frighten them. You may not find this out by asking them, but you will know by the looks on their faces.

As you become more skilled at fighting fairly as a way of resolving conflict, your fights may appear to outside observers as discussions, not fights. This kind of fighting also gives children a model for healthy conflict resolution. In addition, children need assurance that these fights are not an indication that Mom and Dad are going to get a divorce. Some couples make a point of telling their children that it's normal for two people to disagree about things, and that when they fight, they are resolving issues that one or both of them feel strongly about.

When we have healthy fights, we are also showing our children that people who love each other can express anger and resentment directly to one another.

Sample Fighting Contracts

Sample 1:
We agree to the following fighting rules:
- Conducting ourselves honorably.
- Making initial statement of angry feelings about a behavior or situation, but then mutually agreeing to continue to fight.
- Fighting when we will not be interrupted by the kids.
- Finding a place where we can have eye-to-eye contact.
- Refraining from fighting at meal times.
- No blaming.
- No saying, "You always ..." or "You never ..."
- Stopping after 10:00 p.m.; putting the fight on hold till a later time.

Sample 2:
We agree to the following fighting rules:
- No fighting just before or just after work.
- No comparing each other to our respective parents.
- No being critical; no using a hostile tone of voice.

Sample 3:
We agree that our arguments will be confined to the following fighting rules:
- No fighting after 9:00 p.m.
- No shaming statements.
- Setting a time limit, and when that time is up, negotiating for more time.
- No hanging up the phone on each other.
- Stating the focus of the argument.
- Agreeing that this issue is important enough to fight about.

Sample 4:

We hereby establish the following fighting rules:

- No name calling.
- No shaming.
- Use "I feel" statements.
- All time-outs are a minimum of 10 minutes.
- End our arguments within 30 minutes.
- No abusive tone of voice.
- No comparisons allowed (e.g., making references to how we resemble parents or others we know).
- No references to past behavior.

Fighting rules   *Together*

Our fighting rules:

1. _____

2. _____

3. _____

4. _____

5. _____

6. _____

7. _____

8. _____

9. _____

10. _____

11. _____

12. _____

13. _____

14. _____

15. _____

_____   _____
Signature of Partner   Signature of Partner

_____   _____
Signature of Sponsor   Signature of Sponsor

_____
Date

Twelve rules for effective problem solving

One of the things you may have noticed in using this workbook (and by doing Step Seven in particular) is that there are certain problems in your relationship that you seem unable to solve. These problems just persist year after year, in spite of your best efforts to solve them. If necessary, refer to the work you did in Steps One and Four, and in the exercises on intimacy and dependency, for clarification of the issues that persist in your relationship.

Because the capacity to solve problems is closely related to the ability for healthy fighting, poor problem-solving skills often lead to unhealthy fighting. If you have had some practice in having healthy fights, you may want to turn your attention now to one of these problems.

Choose just one of those problems–whether it involves finances, children, trust or sexuality. With this problem in mind, read through the following Twelve rules for problem solving.

No. 67: Major Conflict   *Together*

List the major argument/conflict to which you have chosen to apply the Twelve Steps to problem solving.

_____

_____

_____

_____

_____

Rule 1: Agree on an environment and schedule.

According to your fighting contract, you have realized that there are places that increase the likelihood of your having a healthy fight. There are also places/ways you can have healthy, productive discussions where conflict can be solved with creative solutions. These are places where you feel safe, where there will be no distractions, and where you feel it is relatively easy to express your true feelings about problems and issues.

For example, Phil and LuAnne have found that going away from their kids to a restaurant, even just a fast food joint, enables them to relax and find solutions more quickly.

Rule 2: Identify the issue or concern.

Once you've come together, again ask yourselves

- What the issue or concern really is.
- Why is it a problem?
- What difficulty has it created in your lives?
- What are the components of the problem?
- Can you break it into smaller pieces? For example, perhaps you have a problem with your children. First try to define the main concerns you have. Is it their school performance? Their attitudes toward each other? Their personal discipline? Talking back to you?

Notice the emotions or feelings this problem triggers in you. Does it bring up family-of-origin issues? If so, try to get all these feelings out in the open before you try to solve this problem. In some cases, you may need to get individual help in order to deal with and resolve them. You need to come to some personal resolution before you can continue solving the relationship problem that was affected by these issues.

By going through this process, many problems immediately become more manageable, rather than seeming like amorphous monstrosities that are overwhelming. With this process, problems take on dimensions and aspects which can be dealt with one at a time. You can feel like you are making headway in solving them.

Rule 3: Identify which Step you will need to work on this issue.

Solving the unresolved problems in your relationship depends on your ability to work through certain Steps. If you didn't do the work of Step One, for example, your attempts to solve a problem may drive you so deeply into feelings of despair over your inability to resolve it that you automatically exit the relationship.

Similarly, a problem may have triggered old family-of-origin issues in the past. You may have attempted to deal with it in the unproductive and unhealthy ways you learned while growing up. If you haven't dealt with the family-of-origin issues this problem triggers, you will not be able to get to the core issues involved. Refer again to Rule 2. Perhaps more and deeper dimensions of the problem will reveal themselves to you.

This rule allows you to deal with any guilt or shame you've had in being unable to solve this problem. Working some of the earlier exercises in Step Seven helps you with the communication and conflict resolution skills you need to finally deal with the problem more effectively. Steps Eight and Nine help you ask for the forgiveness of any people you have harmed by not resolving this problem.

Rule 4: Do a personal inventory around the issue of concern.

What is your personal responsibility for the failure to solve this problem? If it is a financial issue, for example, ask yourself if you earn enough money, if you work together to make sure the checkbook balances, or if you avoid the issue entirely.

Look only at your own role; don't take your partner's inventory. How have you contributed to the lack of solutions to this problem?

Rule 5: Name solutions you have tried that haven't worked.

The work required here is similar to the work you did in Step One, but now it is being applied to a specific problem.

Rule 6: Brainstorm all possible solutions.

Be creative here. Don't censor yourselves. The process here is the key. Write down *anything* that comes to mind. You never know when something seemingly outrageous will trigger an effective idea later. Be silly. Have fun with each other. Problem-solving doesn't have to be dull and deadly serious.

Rule 7: Discuss each possible solution.

Okay, now you *do* have to put a reality check on your Rule 6 results. Be careful, too, remembering that you don't have to do this all by yourself. As you review the list you created in Rule 6, you may find it helpful or even necessary to get advice from someone outside your relationship. Perhaps you need to talk to a financial expert for budgeting help, or a child counselor for parenting suggestions. It's okay to ask for help! Being able to ask for help is a sign of healthy intimacy and a healthy relationship.

This rule also offers you the opportunity to practice really listening to each other. Maybe a solution your partner has suggested seems ineffective at first, but becomes feasible after some time and talk. Try not to dismiss any suggestions outright. By listening to one another, you are demonstrating your respect for each other and valuing each other's worth and intelligence.

It's possible for this process to bring up feelings of inadequacy. You may feel, for example, that your partner is simply better at solving problems, that you are inadequate, and that your partner will want to leave you because you can't do this. If you have difficulty listening to your partner's solutions, it may be because of your own feelings of inadequacy rather than the worth of the suggestion. If you feel this way, please share these feelings with your partner.

Rule 8: Agree on one solution or combination of solutions to try.

After the discussion of all possible solutions, you need to agree to try one solution–or a combination of them–before you can move ahead. Keep in mind that this decision isn't etched in stone. If, after some time passes, you find that your solution needs to be amended, return to this process and make changes. But for now, decide on something and go for it!

Rule 9: Create a plan. Decide how each partner will work toward the solution.

Decide on the actions you will take in the days ahead to implement the solution(s) you chose. While your long-range goal is to solve the problem, you may need to take a number of intermediate steps and even daily steps on the way. In your plan, decide what your individual responsibilities are for the solution, and what smaller action steps each of you will take. Write these steps down and hold each other accountable for their accomplishment.

A word of caution: Be wary of black-and-white thinking, believing that your problems will somehow magically evaporate overnight with minimal effort by using this process. Your problems have been around a while, perhaps even years, and their solutions also require time. If through mismanagement of your finances you've incurred a good bit of debt, it may take you a few years to solve this problem.

Rule 10: Contact a couple for feedback on the solution. Revise if necessary.

You previously have been encouraged to seek advice from others , so you may want to contact another couple now for feedback also. They can serve as a sounding board and a reality check for the solutions you've chosen. It may also be that this couple has previously experienced difficulties similar to yours, and discovered effective solutions that can help you. Listen to their comments and revise your plan as necessary.

Rule 11: Agree on a schedule and appropriate environment for ongoing meetings to review the process and your plan.

No plan is perfect for all time. Yours may need revision and updating as time passes and circumstances change. Don't be discouraged or ashamed if you have to make changes. This process encourages trial and error as a way to find solutions to problems.

Rule 12: Affirm each other as you each contribute to the solution.

Long-standing problems in relationships often serve to distract partners from deeper feelings and issues. As you solve and eliminate these problems, you may find that feelings of loneliness, anxiety and fear will surface. If this happens to you, it is important to support and encourage each other for participating in this process. Be gentle with one another. Be honest with each other about your feelings. Implementing each of these rules take practice. You can expect the process to be one of trial and error.

Finally, as you become accustomed to using these rules to work with this first problem, you may want to begin applying them to other problems you have identified in your relationship.

We believe that making contracts with one another to carry out certain rules is important and effective for solving relationship problems. For example, if one of the problems in your relationship is that you believe that you never have enough time to play together, you could make a contract with each other to have regular periods of play.

One couple with this problem hired a babysitter to come to their house every Saturday night at 7 p.m. for six months, no matter what. They agreed that they would leave when the sitter came, whether or not they had figured out what they were going to do.

Another couple who were experiencing sexual difficulties sought help from a counselor. Still another couple was experiencing difficulty talking with each other. They agreed to see a therapist who helped them develop better communication skills. Some partners have made clear contracts with themselves and their children regarding duties and responsibilities around the house such as dish washing, car privileges, arranging for baby sitters.

Learning to communicate

Good communication skills are crucial for developing and maintaining a healthy relationship. As with any other skill, learning them takes time and practice. While working Steps Six and Seven, your ability to communicate will grow if you are rigorous, honest and disciplined with your practice.

Take a time-out now and check your progress. First, are you following the rules we gave you at the beginning of Part One for using this workbook? (See page *xv*)

Second, notice whether you are beginning your statements to each other with the word "I" or the word "you"? The pronoun you are choosing indicates the degree to which you are taking responsibility for your contribution to the health of the relationship. "I" statements indicate responsibility. "You" statements often indicate blaming.

Relationship Tool

Finally, ask yourself whether you are taking enough time to listen to your partner. Do you feel you understand each other's messages? Some of you will have difficulty communicating as you work through this book. If you do, you might try the commonly used communication technique of mirroring. After your partner tells you something, you tell him or her–in different words–what he or she has just said. Your partner can then tell you if you have understood his or her meaning. This technique gives each of you the chance to clarify your statements. It also encourages each partner to give his full attention to the other's statements, rather than planning his own response while the other person is still talking. The result is a give-and-take process that continues until both partners are satisfied they are understood.

Celebrate your courage

Step Six declares that we must be entirely ready to have our Higher Power remove all of our defects of character, communication and caring. If you are experiencing difficulty in working Steps Six and Seven, it may be because you are not "entirely ready." To be ready takes a great deal of courage. Your old ways of being with each other were familiar. They may be extremely dysfunctional, but, if nothing else, they are familiar. There is safety in familiarity. It is hard to give up familiar and safe paths that have built up over time.

Be aware that as you remove these defects of character, communication and caring; deep-seated issues of trust, anxiety, loneliness and sadness readily surface. This can be very frightening, and you may be sorely tempted to return to your old, unhealthy patterns.

Don't be alarmed by this situation. Every couple experiences such highs and lows, and movement forward and backward. Be true to the process, be honest with those helping you, and remind one another that making progress takes courage. Being ready also means being committed to your relationship. It means accepting that if the character defects in your relationship are removed, your partner will be able to fulfill your needs for intimacy.

Praise and congratulate each other in those moments when you realize that one of you has made an honesty breakthrough or taken responsibility for actions in a way not done before. Such breakthroughs take much courage. Acknowledge that fact.

Chapter 8: *Steps Eight and Nine*

STEP EIGHT: We made a list of all persons we had harmed, and became willing to make amends to them all.

STEP NINE: We made direct amends to such people wherever possible, except when to do so would injure them or others.

Through the work of the previous Steps, you already know that your unhealthy behaviors harmed you as a couple. Steps Eight and Nine show you how the dysfunctional parts of your relationship have hurt others as well.

In Step Eight, you continue to take your own inventory as a couple, just as you did in Step Four. Use any of the work you did in Steps One, Six and Seven to help answer this question: "How has our couple dysfunction harmed other people."

In Step Nine, you actually make amends for any harm you caused. Besides asking for help from your Higher Power for your shortcomings, you work as a couple to mend the harm you have caused through your unhealthy and destructive behaviors.

As you work on these two Steps, your amends help you let go of shame and guilt. Recognizing and correcting dysfunctional behavior, combined with making restitution for harm done to each other and others becomes an ongoing part of your life.

Sometimes, in the early work of Step Eight, couples have a difficult time distinguishing between how they hurt others individually and how they did so as a couple. The idea of bringing harm to others as a couple may be new to you.

One couple recalled a conversation their 16-year-old daughter had with friends in which she repeatedly made statements that included such phrases as, "my parents said…" and "my parents made me…" It was clear to them that in their daughter's mind, mother and father were a unit. To her, they had a collective identity and spoke with a unified voice. Many of the people who know you see you as a couple. Think about this collective identity as you work Step Eight. How have you *as a couple* affected others and perhaps harmed them?

In the following exercise, you make a list of those people you feel you have harmed as a couple. As you look into your past, it may help you to think of people in various categories—your children, relatives, neighbors, work colleagues, casual acquaintances.

For many couples, the first people who come to mind are their children. Have you caused any harm to your children?

Consider the following questions.

- Has the dysfunction of your relationship affected your parenting ability?
- In what ways have you failed to provide for the physical, emotional, intellectual or spiritual well-being and health of your children?
- Have you spent enough time with them?
- Have you helped with and supported their academic life?
- Have you provided moral and spiritual guidance for them?
- Have you attended to their physical needs?
- Have you given them the emotional nurturing and guidance they required?

Now turn your attention to others in your lives.

- How have you treated members of your extended family—parents, brothers and sisters, grandparents, nieces and nephews?
- Have you kept in touch with these people?
- Have you offered assistance when they were in need?
- Have you somehow acknowledged important days in their lives, such as birthdays, anniversaries, school graduations?
- Have you shared holidays with them when possible?
- How have you treated those you work with, your neighbors and other acquaintances? There are many ways you could have harmed these people?
- Have you brought your conflicts to public occasions, embarrassing or even insulting your hosts or other guests?
- Did you try to take a "geographic cure" for your relationship troubles, thinking that by moving away you could leave your problems behind?
- Did these sudden moves (which actually parallel "walking out" behavior in relationships) leave employers, work colleagues and friends abruptly cut off and hurt with no explanation as to why you left?
- Did your conflicts impel you to avoid responsibilities to others or to walk out on other relationships, thus creating grief, disappointment, and trouble for those left behind?
- Examine your relationships with other couples and accept any harm you may have created in their relationship.
- Have your conflicts caused you to become overinvolved in their lives?

• Have the ways you socialized encouraged or reinforced the unhealthy behavior of other couples or individuals? We know couples who continually reached out to other couples because of a deep lack of intimacy in their own relationship. In extreme cases, they badly overstepped relationship boundaries, sometimes even to the point of sexual involvement.

No. 68: Couple's Eighth Step   *Together*

As you make your list of the people you have harmed in the **Couple's Eighth Step Worksheet** on page 164, it is important to consider:

Person(s) you've harmed. In the left column, name the people you have harmed as a couple. Think not only of those closest to you, but more casual acquaintances, too.

Nature of harm done. Write down specific details about the harm done, including your behaviors and the other party's reactions. You can include facial expressions, tone of voice, circumstances, and any other details that clarify what happened. Be sure that you consider the ongoing nature and consequences of the harm done. Did it create long-term damage?

Thoughts/Feelings about the harm done.
• What do you and your partner think now about the situation?
• Do you recognize that you have feelings of sadness?
• Do you fear retaliation by those whom you've harmed?
• Do you have a sense that some of your actions brought the loss of friendships?
• Do you experience feelings of guilt based on your spiritual beliefs?

Beware of how you may have felt angry at the people you and your partner harmed in the past, believing that somehow they deserved to be hurt.

Perhaps your children indeed had misbehaved and your punishment was abusive. Perhaps you and your partner felt vindictive toward your parents for ways they harmed you, and subsequently hurt them as you grew older.

Whatever the situation, you nevertheless remain responsible for the hurt you caused. No child or adult, however they may have harmed you, deserves abusive treatment. Steps Eight and Nine do not ask you to sit in judgment of others, deciding whether or not they deserved to be hurt. Instead, these Steps simply ask you to list those you've harmed, to evaluate and accept responsibility for your role in harming them, and to amend that behavior as best you can.

Intentions for making amends. Here you state that you and your partner are willing to make amends to all the people you've harmed. Being "willing" means that you accept your responsibility for the harm done, and that you want to correct that harm where possible.

It is important to look carefully at your willingness to make amends. It can be difficult to determine what you really hope to accomplish by doing this work.

For example, you and your partner may have underlying codependent intentions if you hope that by making amends you will look good to others or prevent retribution. Or perhaps you are making amends only to reduce another's anger at you. You need to be careful that your willingness to make amends is not based on your own selfishness, but rather on your care and concern for others.

We urge you to think of all the possible ways you and your partner could make amends to those on your list. Just because you've listed a way to make restitution for past harm does not necessarily mean that you will carry it out. In some cases, the restitution you'd like to make will be impossible or impractical to carry out. For example, you may not have the financial means to do so, you may lack other needed resources, or the individual or couple in question may have moved or died.

We also urge you to work with your sponsors or another person of your choosing. They can help you evaluate whether you have clear, positive and genuine intentions, and whether your planned amend is practical.

The most important amends

A final thought. Your list of people you've harmed should also include two in particular: the two of you.

The work you have done in the previous Steps should help you see clearly how you've harmed yourselves and your relationship. Using this workbook and trying to change your relationship is in itself a form of amends. You are in the process of changing the way you treat one another and others just as you are healing the hurt in yourselves and others.

When you finish this Step, you'll have a list of all the amends you are willing and able to make. You also may have some blank spaces in this category.

Soul searching takes time

As you can see, Step Eight can be a lengthy, difficult process, one that requires much soul searching. You may not be able to finish your list in only one sitting. Like the work of the previous Steps, take as much time as you need to complete this one. It's not unusual for memories of harm to others to surface at unpredictable times. You may find also that people will come to you to express their feelings of having been harmed by you. You then have to decide whether to agree or disagree that you did harm them, and then add those whom you've harmed to this list. Fill out this list as completely as you can for now.

Your sponsors can be an important source of help in this Step. They can review your progress and help you stay in touch with reality. They can offer different reactions to some of the events you bring up, challenge your intentions or suggest alternative actions.

We remind you that Step Eight is about guilt. We are asking you to recognize and admit to things you've done that you feel guilty about. It's important to remember, however, that guilt is not shame; guilt is the memory of things you've actually done that have harmed other people.

Having feelings of guilt and having harmed others does not mean, in any way, that you are bad people or that you are a bad couple. And it doesn't mean that you don't have tremendous potential for improvement and good. You do! Recognizing legitimate feelings of guilt, however, allows you to deal with situations and often correct them. Being able to reconcile guilt has a great effect in releasing your feelings of shame as months and years pass.

Be extra gentle

At times, couples take on responsibility for actions and events that really don't belong to them in what is known as neurotic guilt.

There may be times when you feel responsible for things that happened in certain situations or to other people when the responsibility doesn't really belong to you. There may be people in your lives who blame you for hurt or damage that they experienced. From a more objective vantage point, their hurt may be their own responsibility or that of others.

Whenever you evaluate your own responsibilities, remember that you have probably lived within circles of people whose relationships and lives included much unhealthy behavior. These people may be good at the practice of blaming. They may want you and your partner to be responsible for their own dysfunctional behavior. They may challenge you to make amends or restitution to them to avoid accepting responsibility for their own behavior and relationships. Be wary of these "guilt peddlers." They would like to sell you their responsibility–and thus have you own it. This is another of the numerous places where it helps you enormously to have outside opinions or evaluations as you work to determine the extent of your responsibility for a given situation.

Remember, too, that many of you are self-centered, perhaps even a bit narcissistic. Your self-evaluation sometimes depends on your belief that you have more power than you actually do. Don't be surprised if you discover this about yourselves.

Many of us grew up in families in which our parents allowed us to believe we were responsible for their well-being in ways that a child should not have to feel responsible. As you may recall in Part One, this is a kind of emotional abuse. It occurs when a parent who should be caring for, nurturing and creating healthy boundaries for a child, instead encourages the child to feel responsible for the parent's care and nurturing.

If you grew up in such a situation, very likely you learned at a very young age (between 2 and 5 years old) to feel responsible for other people's feelings and lives. As an adult, your sense of your own power, ability and importance can be based on an incorrect assumption of your own power.

As you heal from any sense of grandiosity or self-centeredness, take an accurate assessment of your power in a given situation. Do your actions really have the power to hurt a person for the rest of their life? While it is important to discover and accept the things you are truly guilty for, it is equally important to let go of those you do not need to feel guilty about.

Step Eight becomes a way to both accept and let go of responsibility. Working it involves accepting all those things you need to do over the coming months and years to make amends for past harm caused. But it's also a process of letting go of those responsibilities you incorrectly assumed, burdens that trapped you until now.

Step Eight is about making an accurate assessment of what is really your responsibility.

COUPLE'S EIGHTH STEP WORKSHEET

PERSON(S) HARMED:	NATURE OF HARM DONE:
1. _____	_____
_____	_____
2. _____	_____
_____	_____
3. _____	_____
_____	_____
4. _____	_____
_____	_____
5. _____	_____
_____	_____
6. _____	_____
_____	_____
7. _____	_____
_____	_____
8. _____	_____
_____	_____

OUR FEELINGS ABOUT THE HARM DONE:

_____

_____

_____

_____

_____

_____

_____

_____

_____

_____

_____

_____

_____

INTENTIONS FOR MAKING AMENDS:

_____

_____

_____

_____

_____

_____

_____

_____

_____

_____

_____

_____

_____

STEP NINE: We made direct amends to such people wherever possible, except when to do so would injure them or others.

As you move on to Step Nine, it is important to recognize that this Step will be a lifelong process. This is an action Step, the one in which you actually make amends as a couple.

Now you review your list together and decide which amends are the most important and urgent, and which are the most practical to make.

Don't try to take care of all your amends in a few days–they take time. Just as the Twelve Steps tell you to live one day at a time, so, too, it is wise to make your amends one day at a time. Make only those amends for which you and your partner have the ability and maturity.

What does it mean to "make amends"?

The word *amend* has two primary meanings as it is practiced in Twelve Step programs.

First of all, to *amend* means to change. If you and your partner have harmed others, recognize that you need to change the behaviors that caused the harm in the first place and eliminate them from your lives. For example, if you injured someone through inappropriate expressions of anger, seeking to amend that behavior means changing the way you express anger.

The word *amend* also means to make restitution, that is, to repair the damage that was caused. If money has been stolen, for instance, it should be returned. Restitution in the case of emotional harm may mean saying, "We are sorry, we didn't mean to hurt you like that," or "we didn't mean what we said," or "Will you please forgive us?" The simple act of saying, "we are sorry," and the act of forgiveness by the other person(s) or couple(s) can be healing for all concerned.

Emotional healing can also take a long time. In one case, amends were made by paying for the person harmed to get counseling. A word of caution: Not all amends can or should be made by simply saying, "We're sorry." Such amends may be nothing more than an easy way out. For some people, saying "We're sorry" is only a disguised demand for forgiveness: "We're sorry, and you will forgive us, *won't* you." Saying we are sorry is often only the beginning to providing restitution.

Also, recognize that there are some people you've harmed who will never be able to forgive you, or who will never stop judging you for certain actions you and your partner have done. In such cases, no amount of restitution you make will be enough to satisfy them. At some point, you have to decide that you've done the best you can to amend a given situation, and let go of it.

When amends can't be made directly, many couples we know have found it helpful to make what we call vicarious restitution. By this we mean doing something for a person who symbolically represents the one you actually harmed. For example, if you caused emotional hurt but paying for the individual's counseling expenses is impractical or inappropriate, you could instead pay counseling expenses for someone who's been similarly harmed. If it's no longer possible to repay a person from whom you have stolen money, you could contribute a like amount to charity.

"One dime at a time."

Debtors Anonymous saying

Making vicarious amends can also remind you that you are not making amends just to heal the damage in those you've harmed. It also heals the hurt you've caused yourselves through the guilt you carry. Even if an amend is only symbolic, it may help greatly in healing some of your guilt.

Most important, take action *only* when doing so will not harm anyone else. It is important to think about the effect of your amend on those involved before you move ahead with it. Perhaps making amends requires more honesty than the other party can handle. Sometimes trying to correct behavior or make restitution can injure another, or the person(s) may not want to see or talk to you. If contact triggers memories of pain and hurt in them, then the amend would be destructive and should not be made. .

In other cases, raising old issues may cause someone involved to learn about a past action or event, thus violating anonymity and leading to hurt. If you had an affair with someone, for example, and making amends might mean that their spouse would learn of it for the first time, then the amend should not be made, even though you are willing to do so.

The work of making amends will often require great creativity on your part. The examples of other couples who've recovered and made amends to those they've harmed can be helpful to you as you work this Step.

Check amends with your sponsors

In working through this Step, it is strongly recommended that you turn to your sponsors for advice about when an amend is appropriate. It's not unusual for people to be overly zealous in making amends and anxious to complete them in order to be forgiven by those harmed. Your own needs to be forgiven should never lead you to act too quickly. It's important to act carefully, prudently and wisely. Again, ask for help from your sponsors or others you trust.

No. 69: Couple's Ninth Step

As you make amends in the coming weeks, months and years, record them on the Couple's Ninth Step worksheet below.

- In the **Person(s) Harmed** column, name those you've harmed.

- In the **Amends Made** column, record the way you carried out your amend.

- Under **Results**, record the results of your amend. Was it well received? Did it result in the desired reaction? Did restitution take place? Was forgiveness expressed? Did healing seem to happen?

- Under **Our Feelings**, record what you felt as a couple during the process. Were you frightened as you began the amend? What were you afraid of? Were you worried about what the person's reaction would be? About what they would say? That you wouldn't be forgiven?
  As the amend progressed, did you feel brave? Did you find that working together as a couple was enjoyable? Did you get affirmation from one another for having moved ahead and actually doing this together?
  What did you feel when the amend was complete? Relief? Peace? That it went well? Sadness? Frustration? What did you learn from the process that could be helpful in creating and carrying out future amends?

- In the **Date** column, simply record the date of the amend, and have it initialed by your sponsors. By so doing, they witness that the amend was completed.

Again, remind yourselves that you are making amends not only for others but for yourselves.

Gentleness reminder

Working through Steps Eight and Nine can leave you with some difficulty seeing the difference between your guilt and your feelings of shame. Remind yourselves that you have done the best that you could given the way you were raised and the models you had for relationships.

Even if you damaged yourselves or others over time, you are encouraged to recognize that because you've hurt someone doesn't mean you are a bad person. Be easy on yourselves. Take a gentleness break and do something special for yourselves.

SAMPLE WORKSHEET

PERSON(S) HARMED:	AMENDS MADE:	RESULTS:	OUR FEELINGS:	DATE:
1. **Our daughter**	We want to say we are sorry for times we abandoned her or were inappropriately angry with her. We promise to deal more appropriately with our anger and spend more time with her in the future.	She understood and accepted our apology; said she wanted a better relationship with us in the future; all present cried and hugged one another.	Sadness over lost opportunities to be better parents to her earlier in her life; relief that she accepted our apology; joy and excitement that we will be able to work toward a better relationship with her in the future.	

COUPLE'S NINTH STEP WORKSHEET

PERSON(S) HARMED:	AMENDS MADE:
1.	
2.	
3.	
4.	
5.	
6.	
7.	
8.	

RESULTS:	OUR FEELINGS:	DATE:

Chapter 9: *Steps Ten, Eleven and Twelve*

STEP TEN: We continued to take a personal inventory, and when we were wrong, promptly admitted it to our partner and to others we had harmed.

STEP ELEVEN: We sought through our common prayer and meditation to improve our conscious contact with God as we understood God, praying only for knowledge of God's will for us and the power to carry that out.

STEP TWELVE: Having had a spiritual awakening as the result of these Steps, we tried to carry this message to other couples and to practice these principles in all aspects of our lives, our relationship and our families.

As part of your ongoing recovery, these final three Steps focus on practicing what you have learned in the first nine Steps. Steps Ten and Eleven ask you to draw on the early principles and work of this book. They ask you to integrate the program principles of honesty and spiritual exploration into your daily life as a couple.

We have emphasized the need for balance, focus and self-responsibility throughout this workbook. Applying these concepts to the final three Steps means:

Balance–acknowledging your personal and couple strengths and weaknesses.

Focus–regularly taking your inventory, both as an individual and as a couple.

Self-responsibility–promptly acknowledging your successes and failures as a couple.

Regular, realistic monitoring of your strengths and weaknesses, and a willingness to acknowledge your failures and successes reinforces your progress. By making a commitment as a couple to integrity and honesty, you lay the foundation for a spirituality that will infuse your everyday life. Conversely, rigorous self-examination can only be sustained with a strong spiritual base, which is Step Eleven. The combination of the two can become a way of life for you as a couple.

STEP TEN: We continued to take a personal inventory, and when we were wrong, promptly admitted it to our partner and to others we had harmed.

This Step can be divided into two main parts. The first involves a continued examination of the effect your individual behaviors have on each other; the second involves continued monitoring of the effects your behavior as a couple has on others in your lives.

No. 70: Couple's Weekly Inventory *Individual*

The following exercise helps you carry out the first part of this Step. On the following page is the Couple's Weekly Inventory worksheet.

Find a quiet place where you can each be by yourself. Then, for 15 or 20 minutes, think about anything you did during the past week that was not helpful or that was harmful to your relationship.

Questions you might ask yourself include:

- What old patterns of dysfunction did I maintain?
- Did I say or do things that were cruel or harmful or not helpful?
- Did I fail to comply with any commitments or agreements that I made?
- Did I fail to fulfill some of my individual responsibilities?

Write your answers in the left column, "My Behaviors That Were Not Helpful."

To fill out the right column, "Your Gifts to Me," think about the things your partner did for you during the past week that you found helpful and that you appreciated–either large or small. In this list, you also may include things your partner didn't do that you found helpful. Perhaps, for example, your partner stopped nagging you about something, and you found a great sense of relief that he had stopped!

As you work through this exercise, relax and let your mind bring examples to your consciousness. After 15 or 20 minutes, you may have only one or two items in each column, or 20 or 30. Don't have any expectations about how many you should have. Whatever comes to you is fine.

COUPLE'S WEEKLY INVENTORY

MY BEHAVIORS THAT WERE NOT HELPFUL:	YOUR GIFTS TO ME:

1. _____

_____

2. _____

_____

3. _____

_____

4. _____

_____

5. _____

_____

6. _____

_____

7. _____

_____

8. _____

_____

When each of you has completed your list, come back together and exchange them.

Take care the first few times you do this exercise. As you exchange and read each other's lists for the first time, you may be tempted to add to your partner's list. If you feel, for example, that your partner forgot to mention something kind that you'd done, you are not allowed to say, "Well, you forgot that I…"

If your partner has not mentioned something in his/her list that you believe was harmful to you, likewise, you are not allowed to bring up this issue. This is not an exercise in adding to lists. Simply exchange and read them. You may, however, ask for clarification on any point, saying, for example, "What did you mean when you said I…?"–but no more.

Once you've looked over and clarified one another's lists, the exercise is finished. When you have done this exercise a few times, you may want to spend more time talking to each other and reaffirming the positive and helpful things you did for one another.

Those of you who have previously worked a 12-step program may recognize that filling out the left column is, in a sense, a part of your individual Eighth Step. You recognize that you did certain unhelpful things during the past week, and you make amends and try to change.

The work of this inventory is intended to fulfill three basic goals:

The first is to reverse the process of blame. Again, you are challenged to take personal responsibility for the unhealthy and unproductive behaviors in your relationship, to make amends for it, and to change in the future. Those of you who feel a good deal of discomfort with this exercise should look at just how much your blaming behavior has affected the way you relate to your partner.

Second, relationships thrive when partners regularly affirm one another. Supporting and affirming each other is a way of nourishing and building each other up. The experiences of many couples show that as partners begin to do this, blaming decreases. Individual feelings of shame diminish as well, as each learns that they are truly loved and appreciated by their partner. Hearing your partner's affirmations about your helpful behaviors helps you understand, perhaps for the first time, what your partner likes and appreciates. This exercise also offers an opportunity to encourage one another to do things for each other that are truly pleasing.

Third, we have all grown up within an environment–a family of origin, a society and a peer group–that taught us particular ways to please a partner. Men have often been led to believe, for example, that as long as they provide income and shelter for their partner, they have no other responsibilities in meeting their partner's needs.

Often women in our culture have been taught that if they keep up the house, take care of the children, cook and occasionally take part in sex, they have fulfilled their responsibilities to their partner.

You will learn by doing this exercise over the coming weeks and months that some of your culturally based assumptions are incorrect. This exercise may also help you understand why, if you held such beliefs, your partner was not satisfied with your efforts.

In the Recovering Couples Anonymous fellowship, countless couples say that this particular exercise has been helpful in reversing the process of blame and anger they have experienced in their relationships.

No. 71: Improvements   *Together*

First, recall what you learned in Steps Eight and Nine and continue to review these Steps. Now focus on your amends: what are you doing to ensure that you are not continuing to harm other people.

As you make your ongoing relationship inventory, you will recognize that there are times when you repeat harm done in the past. When you realize this, these incidents should be added to your Eighth Step list and considered for amends in your Ninth Step.

It is equally important when taking a moral inventory to pay attention to the things you've done well. In this exercise, list areas in your life in which you feel you have made improvements. A number of broad categories of ways in which your relationship may have improved are listed in this exercise.

A. Ways we are communicating better.

1. _____

2. _____

3. _____

4. _____

5. _____

B. Ways we are reversing the problem of blaming one another.

1. _____

2. _____

3. _____

4. _____

5. _____

C. Ways we are better able to communicate anger and resentment, and are able to have fair fights.

1. _____

2. _____

3. _____

4. _____

5. _____

D. Ways we are amending our individual behaviors so as not to harm our partner.

1. _____

2. _____

3. _____

4. _____

5. _____

E. Ways we are being better parents.

1. _____

2. _____

3. _____

4. _____

5. _____

F. Ways we are being better friends.

1. _____

2. _____

3. _____

4. _____

5. _____

G. Ways we are improving in our work environment.

1. _____

2. _____

3. _____

4. _____

5. _____

H. Ways we are learning to play together better.

1. _____

2. _____

3. _____

4. _____

5. _____

The categories presented above to help you make an ongoing inventory of your relationship are a way to help you give yourselves credit for the positive changes you are bringing to your relationship.

You are invited to add your own categories. List other ways you see your relationship improving.

You might also refer to the Intimacy and Dependency scale exercises you worked in Steps Six and Seven. Re-examine the categories described there. Do you see any improvements in your relationship in the areas of healthy intimacy and healthy dependency? If so, please note them here as well.

I. Examples of ways

1. _____

2. _____

3. _____

4. _____

5. _____

J. Examples of ways

1. _____

2. _____

3. _____

4. _____

5. _____

K. Examples of ways

1. _____

2. _____

3. _____

4. _____

5. _____

Take a Celebration Break

As part of the work of Step Ten, you are now encouraged to decide on a time and place to celebrate with each other the fact that your relationship is indeed improving.

Go out to dinner and then spend the night at a hotel.

Take a vacation together.

Go for a long walk in a beautiful and quiet natural setting.

Return to a setting that was significant in your courtship.

Use your imagination!

STEP ELEVEN: We sought through our common prayer and meditation to improve our conscious contact with God as we understood God, praying only for knowledge of God's will for us and the power to carry that out.

In the first part of this Step, you are asked to assess the progress of the Spiritual Quest Contract you agreed upon in Step Three. Later, you will look at ways you can better work together to sustain a spiritual life that is both inspiring and fulfilling, and then to incorporate these changes in your Spiritual Quest Contract.

As you work through this Step, please keep in mind that your spiritual quest is an ongoing, lifelong journey. Changes in your spiritual perspective, and in the role it plays in your life, may not seem so immediate and dramatic as some of the other changes you are making in your relationship. For this reason, please do not to discount any changes and improvements you've made, no matter how insignificant they may seem to you right now.

To prepare for this Step, take a moment to go back and review the work you did for both Steps Two and Three.

Now, to help you examine the progress of your spiritual quest, ask yourselves the following questions and answer those you are able to.

• **What parts of your Spiritual Quest Contract have you found to be most beneficial?**

_____

_____

• **What parts of your Spiritual Quest Contract have you found to be most difficult to fulfill?**

_____

_____

In Steps Two and Three we discussed how family-of-origin issues can affect an individual's spiritual life. Your religious experience as a child still has an emotional impact on you as an adult even if you have chosen a new religious/spiritual path. You may, for example, find yourself becoming uncomfortable or even angry with your partner's form of religious practice, even though you approve of it intellectually. You may find yourself feeling sad, lonely, uneasy or empty about your spiritual life. If so, you are encouraged to continue talking about it with your partner and find someone who can act as a counselor for spiritual matters to help you.

Are there any issues from your past which seem to interfere with your growing spiritual life?

No. 72: Step Eleven   Together

If you have had difficulty working this Step thus far–perhaps being unable to reach any spiritual common ground–take some time to talk about this.

To help you work through the questions, concerns and problems that come up as you work these first exercises, you may want to use the Twelve Steps for Problem Solving outlined in Step Seven.

You may also want to talk to couples who are managing to deal with spirituality even though they come from different backgrounds or now hold different perspectives. How did they reach a point of common ground or otherwise find peace with their spiritual journey?

Now ask yourselves these questions:

- Have you and your partner encountered any points of conflict over spiritual matters that are interfering with your spiritual growth?
- Have you felt anger with each other about these disagreements?
- Have you felt that your partner has been judgmental about your beliefs?
- Have you felt that your partner has been preaching to you about his or her own beliefs?

Often, anger arises over a concern or belief that one's partner will not "find salvation" if she doesn't accept one's own beliefs. As you talk, try to discover any fears you may have about a failure to come to common ground in this area.

Notes from this discussion:

_____

_____

_____

If you've experienced conflict in this area, or if it's been a struggle for either of you individually, don't lose heart. A spiritual quest is a lifetime journey. The work of Step Eleven is one of slow growth, and the exercises that follow help facilitate and enhance your journey.

The first part of this Step is about seeking. This is the quest you have been encouraged to undertake. The phrase "common prayer and meditation" refers to your spiritual life together as a couple. Later, as part of the ongoing nature of working Step Eleven, look at ways you might want to revise your Spiritual Quest Contract.

No. 73: Conscious Contact *Together*

This exercise is designed to help you think more about what many call conscious contact with the Higher Power as you understand it. Which, for many people, is difficult to think about, much less talk about.

Some people believe they have experienced such contact and communication with their Higher Power. Others point to events in their lives that, while on the surface seeming coincidental, in fact demonstrate the work of a Higher Power in their lives. People report having had conscious contact in a variety of settings: while praying, reading scripture, meditating, listening to music, walking in a beautiful natural setting or during a religious service. Some people report having had mystical experiences in which they believe they heard or saw their Higher Power.

"I walked over to a bridge across the river and the wind was really strong and it was blowing my hair back and the sun was shining and the water was sparkling with the sun and I started crying tears of joy. I knew my Higher Power was with me. I knew I was forgiven. It took probably most of my shame away."

Barb, recovering sex addict

This is not to define the ways in which you or others may come in conscious contact with your Higher Power. But you are asked to answer for yourselves: Have you, either individually or as a couple, felt like you have had conscious contact with a Higher Power? If so, describe that in the space below. Whatever your experiences, simply write them down and then share them with your partner.

Our experiences of conscious contact with the Higher Power.

Partner 1:

_____

_____

_____

_____

Partner 2:

_____

_____

_____

_____

_____

No. 74: Purpose *Together*

Step Eleven tells us to pray for knowledge of our Higher Power's will for us. This statement implies a theology which suggests that a Higher Power does indeed exist, and that this Higher Power plays a crucial and guiding role in helping each of us live our lives. And it raises a further question: How do we blend our Higher Power's help for our individual lives with help for us as a couple?

For some of you, these may be new ideas. Others may recognize them more easily, depending on the religious traditions from which you come. The awareness of a Higher Power working in your life may be difficult for some of you–but it will become a greater part of your life over the coming months and years.

Talk with each other about your individual understandings of this concept of a Higher Power who is involved in your life.

- Do you have a sense of purpose in your life?
- Have either of you ever felt that God or a Higher Power is in your life?
- How do you feel you are doing in regards to accomplishing your life's purpose?
- Do you believe that a Higher Power has a purpose for you as a couple?

Record your comments in the space below.

_____

_____

_____

_____

_____

No. 75: Examples *Together*

Think about any couples you know who seem to be

- accomplishing meaningful work
- fulfilling inner goals that have little to do with material acquisition or career advancement
- dedicated to serving others
- leading lives with an inner harmony, a base note of contentment and deep fulfillment.

If you know couples like this, you may, as part of your Spiritual Quest Contract, want to seek one of them out and spend some time talking with them.

- Do they in fact feel this sense of inner harmony and fulfillment that you see in them?
- What is the basis for it?
- How have they experienced this?
- How do they foster and support it in their daily lives?
- What is their concept of a Higher Power?
- Do they believe they have had conscious contact with a Higher Power?

By speaking to such couples you will also foster greater fellowship around these important questions. Record your answers below, or otherwise summarize what you learned from your conversations.

_____

_____

_____

_____

_____

Suggestions for sustaining a spiritual life

The following exercises will help you develop and choose ways to enhance your spiritual life.

No. 76: Participate in a Spiritual Community   *Together*

By asking you to seek out and speak with couples who might be role models for your spiritual quest, you are encouraged to participate in a spiritual community.

In your past, you may have been part of such a community through your synagogue, church, parish, or mosque. More broadly defined, a spiritual community is a group of people who come together around specific spiritual goals and beliefs. Perhaps you are currently participating in an institutionalized form of religious expression.

As you saw in Steps Two and Three, people have different approaches to creating a spiritual life together. Regardless of how you choose to do this, you are encouraged to participate in regular fellowship with couples who are, like you, on a spiritual quest. This might take place during meetings with other couples in a couples group. You may choose to attend religious services and participate in the community of an organized religion. Some couples have even chosen to live in a religious community with other like-minded couples. Participation in such a spiritual community can be particularly important for people who were raised in dysfunctional families because such communities can serve as models for giving love and nurturing in a family setting.

What plans do you have as a couple to seek, foster and encourage spiritual community in your lives?

_____

_____

_____

_____

_____

No. 77: Agreement on the Ultimate *Together*

Often, the most powerful investment people have in their beliefs concerns what happens to them after they die. Many people believe that if they embrace a correct form of religious expression, it will have an ultimate effect on their lives. Many people believe, for example, that following the tenets of Christianity will result in everlasting life after death.

The following exercise is designed to help you discuss such issues by focusing on the "final things."

First, spend some time individually planning your own funeral. As a way to get started, you might consider the following questions:

- Do you have a will?
- Do you know where you want to be buried, or do you want to be cremated?
- What religious rituals do you want held at your funeral?
- What hymns or other types of music do you want used?
- What do you want to have people read–passages from the Bible, the Koran, the Old Testament, or other books?
- If you want a clergyperson to address the gathering, what would you like this person to say about you and your life?

Imagine, if you were to die today, who would be at your funeral.

_____

_____

_____

When you both have done this individually, compare what you've written with each other. You may notice significant areas of disagreement. If so, do not try to solve them immediately. Just note that you have found an area of significant disagreement that you need to address at some time.

Writing your own mission statement

In the following exercise, you write your own mission statement. That means asking yourselves such questions as: What are you living for? Why are you alive? What are your goals in life?

Seldom do people sit down with the purpose of addressing such questions. Instead, many people just live day-to-day–all the while making decisions, and in fact, creating a life. Yet they have no overall sense of direction.

When we stop long enough to address questions about the meaning and goals of our lives, we can state them. This is what you are now asked to do: to write a mission statement for your lives. When you write out such a statement, you will find that the very act of putting it down on paper creates a kind of impetus to live it out. It's down in black and white; you and others can see the statements. It's no longer in the realm of mind; it's concrete, it's in the world.

No. 78: Mission Statement *Individual*

The first part of this exercise is to write your own mission statement.

Find a place where each of you can be alone and undisturbed, and write your mission statement. You may have already discovered that certain places help you in your attempts to do more contemplative tasks such as this–a quiet setting outside, in a church, in a room with special music. In your heart you know the best place for you.

Be patient. You may find that this is a difficult task, one that takes more than one sitting to accomplish. Take as much time as you need to think about these issues and to write them down in the space below. Seek support for your efforts as you need it. You may even consider going away for a day or a weekend to do this exercise–to write down what you stand for and believe in.

You can put your mission statement in a personal shorthand; you don't have to write volumes. You may just want to get down some key words that represent major concepts or life goals.

Here's an example of what one person wrote:

> To see the truth.
> To speak the truth.
> To be most fully myself.
> To parent well.
> To love sincerely.
> To connect with all.
> To take responsibility for harm.
> To live intentionally.
> To press beyond expectations yet remain within my humanness.
> To protect, guide and nurture all children.
> To carry my ancestors well and reverently.
> To keep confidences of others, yet not participate in secrets or violate my privacy.
> To care for my body.
> To be true to this covenant.

Mission Statement: Partner One

_____

_____

_____

_____

_____

Mission Statement: Partner Two

_____

_____

_____

_____

_____

The second half of Step Eleven helps you seek the will of the Higher Power *for your relationship.* How do you blend your individual missions? At this point, stop and ask yourselves: Now that you have a clearer sense of your individual purpose in life, have you ever felt angry or resentful of your partner because he or she seems to be working at cross-purposes to you? If this is true, be gentle with one another. How would your partner know your purpose or mission if she or he had never been told what it was.

Now that you each have a written statement of your purpose, share them. Notice the points of purpose you hold in common. These points will form the foundation of your joint mission statement.

Next, write a joint mission statement. Just as you did individually, you may need to take a good bit of time to write it. You may even want to go away for a weekend to do this—at a hotel or retreat house, for example. As you develop a joint mission statement, you will find that you have points in common and points of difference in which you will need to act independently of one another.

When you have finished, you are urged to "publish" these statements.
- Print or write them on a separate sheet of paper and post them where others can see and read them–your children, friends, family.
- If your children are grown and away from home, send them a copy and explain what it means.
- If you attend a couples meeting, show it there.
- Give a copy to your sponsors.

A value isn't really a value unless you proclaim it publicly. How will you declare your values?

Joint Mission Statement

_____

_____

_____

_____

_____

No. 79: Setting Life Priorities as a Way of Living Your Values   *Together*

When you have finished your mission statement, examine the priorities in your lives. Are you living those priorities? Is your lifestyle helping you fulfill your life's mission? Are you living together in the way that you want to?

To help you determine the answers to these questions, consider keeping track of how you spend your time for a few weeks, in a general rather than minute-by-minute way. This is more than a time-management exercise.

An easy way to do this is to photocopy a few weeks of blank pages from a daily appointment calendar. Rather than putting in appointments you have to keep, jot down what you do each day.

Do all your activities add to the fulfillment of either your personal or common missions? If not, you are faced with the challenge of giving up those which do not add to your mission.

You may find you're unable to fulfill all your dreams. It takes courage to face this reality, and you will undoubtedly feel grief in letting go and in confronting limitations in your time and in what you can accomplish.

You may also have newfound feelings of relief and empowerment. You have worked through this book, and now many parts of your lives–individually and as a couple–are coming into focus. You are finding a new sense of direction. Because your relationship is better, you have more energy to direct toward your goals, energy that in the past was dissipated in fruitless and unproductive struggles. Your mission as you see it is becoming clearer, giving your lives a new and deeper sense of meaning and direction.

No. 80: Merging Your Mission and Your Spiritual Quest

Together   As the final part of Step Eleven, reconsider your Spiritual Quest Contract. There need not be (and some would say, should not be) a separation between your spiritual quest and what you do in your day-to-day life. So one reason to write a mission statement is to clarify what you are trying to accomplish in your life, to develop and define your spiritual quest.

You may want to include some form of daily spiritual discipline, such as meditation, tai chi or reading to one another. Can you find a way to create time for individual spiritual work to take place in your relationship?

You may decide to contract to do some new activity, something neither of you has ever done before, and to do so on a daily basis.

What changes do you want to make in your Spiritual Quest Contract? You may want to include specific steps to ensure that you are living up to your life's mission as you have just stated it. If one of your mission goals is to be better parents, for example, you may set up a way to spend more time with your children.

Your Spiritual Quest Contract will continue to grow in length and in the nature of its detail as you continue to work Step Eleven.

Revised Spiritual Quest Contract

_____

_____

_____

_____

_____

_____

_____

_____

_____

STEP TWELVE: Having had a spiritual awakening as the result of these Steps, we tried to carry this message to other couples and to practice these principles in all aspects of our lives, our relationship and our families.

Step Twelve is meant to be lived for a lifetime. In the previous eleven, you have been building the foundation needed to experience this Step.

Step Twelve assumes that you have had a spiritual awakening in your lives. Don't be put off by that term. It doesn't necessarily mean having had a dramatic, overwhelming, mystical experience. You may have had such an experience, but for most people, a spiritual awakening means a gradual process of developing intimacy with a Higher Power and with one another.

Awakening also means a rebirth or resurrection. Through your work in the first 11 Steps, you will recognize that your relationship has been in many ways reborn or resurrected. You are experiencing a new life together as a couple. Your feelings for each other and for your relationship may have been near death, but now you have breathed new life into it. Feelings of love and caring for one another have returned and are growing. The amount of emotional, physical and spiritual intimacy in your lives is increasing, too. There has literally been an awakening of intimacy, and this awakening itself is a spiritual event, a spiritual awakening.

If you feel that doing the work of this Step is too difficult for you at this time, that's okay. It is, after all, the final Step. Much preparation and work must be done to be ready for this Step, and that takes time. You will work through this Step when you are ready, and you will know when that time has come.

When you look back on where you and your relationship were when you began this process, the changes you've made in your lives seem remarkable! If you haven't taken a celebration break in the last two weeks or so, put this book down and go plan one!

Carrying the message

The Twelfth Step requires that you share your path with others. The joy of your new life together and its life-giving reality are what you have to give.

Couples react in various ways to the request that they begin carrying the message to other couples. As a couple, you may have felt coupleshame in the past. You may still be carrying feelings that you are just not a good enough couple, and that you don't have much to talk about to another couple. Some of you may feel that you don't know how to talk to other couples or that you lack social skills. Some of you may have been caregivers for much of your lives, and you may have a gut reaction of not wanting to carry *anything* to anyone else.

Telling others about this process never fails to help those who do so. As you teach others, your own understanding of this process grows deeper. As you teach others, you become more proficient in practicing these principles in all aspects of your lives. Furthermore, many couples have found that the more they give away, the more they get back. This phenomenon is one of life's paradoxes, and in fact is one of those spiritual realities that seems so enigmatic until it is experienced.

Think about the ways you can carry this message of recovery to others. Here are some suggestions:

Live the Twelve Steps

You are, in fact, already carrying the message. How? The changes you have made in your relationship will be obvious to others. They may remember you as a couple on the verge of divorce, and now they find you laughing, smiling and talking together. They will sense your newfound peace and joy, and know something has changed. This is carrying the message. We teach others by the example of our lives.

Answer others' questions

Another effective means of carrying the message is simply to answer questions and respond to comments from people who ask you about the changes they see in your relationship and in your lives. If you are living your recovery, the serenity it brings is obvious. You can be certain that others will notice the changes in your relationship and ask how you managed this change. This is a wonderful opportunity to share your story.

Some of you may have a burning desire to tell family members, other relatives, friends, work associates, the whole world what a wonderful difference this work has made in your lives. You may be tempted to "save" every relationship that seems to be in need of repair.

Be careful how you direct this enthusiasm. Think for a moment how you would have felt during the height of your difficulties if another couple had told you that they had the answer to your problems and that they wanted to give it to you. You may have listened politely, or simply told them to get lost. When people are searching for answers, they ask questions. Be sensitive to others. It's not your job to save anyone, or to push your story on anyone who hasn't asked to hear it.

We can learn from the story of Bill W., one of the co-founders of Alcoholics Anonymous. After years of struggle (with the input of Dr. Bob, the other co-founder of AA) Bill had finally found sobriety through using what would become the Twelve Steps of AA He rushed off to the bordellos and bars of New York City, and dragged home the worst alcoholics he could find. He talked to them at great length, trying to convince them to try this new path to sobriety he had found. But his efforts were in vain. These people weren't interested in or ready to hear his message. You may find, like Bill W., that the couples who are ready to hear your message will seek you out; you need not seek them out.

Many couples have found that when they open up about their problems, people respond in kind, telling about their struggles and difficulties. It is almost as though they are thankful for the opportunity to talk about this part of their lives and relieved that someone else understands.

In the early days of Recovering Couples Anonymous, several couples hesitated about sharing the nature of the sexual difficulties they had in their relationships. One couple in a meeting courageously chose to speak of their problems. They found that every other couple in the room was experiencing similar, if not identical, difficulties.

As you tell your story to others, you undoubtedly will have similar experiences. Seldom has a couple been judged for telling their story, or simply been ignored or left for doing so.

Sharing through a fellowship of other couples

Find a group of couples with whom you can regularly meet. This is, in fact, how RCA was founded. It was not formed by couples who wanted to preach the message. The founding couples came together because of their mutual need to have a regular, weekly connection with others who were also working to improve their relationship. They needed this fellowship to support and maintain the changes they were making in their relationships. In the coming weeks and months, carrying the message may simply mean attending meetings, or working to found one. (See Resources for the names, addresses and phone numbers of fellowships.)

Through your participation in a fellowship, you will have the opportunity to tell your story, and thus carry the message. Other couples will see that they are not alone in their struggles. These small acts of sharing create the dynamic energy that makes fellowships so helpful and inspiring, and that carries the message of recovery forward. Never underestimate the power your story can have on the lives of others.

The importance of participating regularly in such a group is without parallel.

No. 81: Step Twelve Strategies   *Together*

List the strategies you will take as a couple to find an existing fellowship or to found one of your own. Review this plan with your sponsors.

_____

_____

_____

_____

_____

Sponsor another couple

As time passes, you may find that another couple asks you to be their sponsor couple. While to do so is both an honor and a privilege, sponsoring another couple needs to wait for another year or two. Sponsorship requires a certain degree of serenity and peace in one's relationship. Your own sponsors can help you decide if you are ready to assume this role.

Being sponsors may sound intimidating to you, but the tasks of a sponsor couple are really quite few:

- Work hard to understand the whole story of the couple you're sponsoring.

- Support them emotionally during the difficult times they will inevitably face.

- Teach them about the basics of RCA

- Help them focus on the Steps of the program.

- Be honest about how you see them working this program.

In your relationship with those you sponsor, look for and point out the positive aspects of their relationship that they are overlooking. (Remember how at times all you could see was disaster.) Help them see what they are doing right. Perhaps the most precious gift a sponsor can give is such beginning affirmations.

As sponsors to other couples, you serve as special role models. How you live the Twelve Steps has a significant effect on those you help. You can get help in learning to help others if you need to.

Carrying the message to other couples does not mean you have to be available to all others at all times. Hopefully, one skill you've learned through the course of this workbook is setting healthy boundaries for yourself. In the recovery process, you undoubtedly will meet a number of the many needy couples who are seeking help. You don't have to tell your story to everyone who comes along, and you don't have to sponsor every couple who asks. This further points out the need and value of having a fellowship of couples with whom you can share this work. Be wary of letting your recovery become just another form of workaholism. While giving service is clearly important, you can't serve well unless you are taking care of yourselves and your recovery first.

In practicing the Twelfth Step, you will find that:

- By telling other couples about your experiences, your appreciation of the program and the program's impact on your life will deepen.

- By hearing the stories of other couples, you are reminded of where you were when you started.

- By modeling to other couples, you become aware that you need to practice what you preach.

- By giving to other couples, you become aware that you need to practice what you preach.

- By helping other couples, you give back what you have received.

- By supporting others' beginning steps, you revitalize your own efforts.

If you followed the suggestions for working this book, you have had sponsors who have supported you throughout these exercises. Remember how important they were to you in your lives. As you grow in peace and serenity in this program, you will find yourselves able to give these gifts to others.

As a final act of celebration, do something special for your sponsors.

Practicing the principles

Step Twelve encourages you to practice these principles in all aspects of your lives, relationships and families. When you successfully work on Steps Ten, Eleven and Twelve, the skills that you build and develop for yourselves not only affect your relationship with your partner, but also enhance your ability to live in the world and to have relationships with others, including those in your family. As a couple, you become better parents, better friends, better family members and better workers.

For example, the ability to take responsibility for your own behavior, rather than blaming others, has a great affect on how peacefully you live. This ability also helps you take responsibility for improving your life.

One final word of caution is important. The experiences of many recovering individuals and couples have found that the peace and serenity of the program and the improvement in one's life may not take place in the first weeks or months of recovery. If your lives together as a couple have been quite problem-filled, the consequences of those behaviors may affect you for some time after you have begun this program. If this happens, try not to be discouraged. Any ongoing consequences can be interpreted and used as reminders of how difficult your lives were before you began following this 12-step program. Use them, too, as encouragement to follow these Steps rigorously.

Your relationship with your children can bring ongoing consequences that are quite painful. The unhealthy aspects of your relationship have undoubtedly had a significant impact on them, as well as others around you. The effect may have lifetime consequences. Just as many of us were parented in unhealthy ways, so too we may have already parented our children in a similar fashion. Throughout this workbook, you are encouraged to be gentle with yourselves. Everyone makes mistakes and repeats patterns from the past.

As you practice the principles of these Twelve Steps, you will begin making changes that have ongoing positive effects on your children and others around you. There will still be times when memories of past unhealthy behavior will surface and trigger both of you into old feelings of despair. Don't be discouraged. Each of us in recovery goes through this experience of highs and lows.

You may also see other vestiges of ongoing damage. Some may affect your financial life together, others may affect your career opportunities, or old friendships, or your sexual life together. Do not try to solve any of these problems once and for all by working these Twelve Steps this first time. These issues and others like them—children, finances, sexuality, career, and so on—will be addressed in greater depth in future supplements to this book. We encourage you to work on them in the future when it feels comfortable. ❦

The Promises

If we are honest about our commitment and painstaking about working the Twelve Steps together, we will quickly be amazed at how soon our love returns. We are going to know a new freedom and a new happiness. We will learn how to play and have fun together. As we experience mutual forgiveness, we will not regret the past nor wish to shut the door on it. Trust in each other will return. We will comprehend the word serenity, and we will know peace.

No matter how close to brokenness we have come, we will see how our experiences can benefit others. That feeling of uselessness, shame and self-pity will disappear. We will lose interest in selfish things and gain interest in our partners, families and others. Self-seeking will slip away. Our whole attitude and outlook on life will change. Fear of people and of economic insecurity will leave us. We will intuitively know how to handle situations which used to baffle us. We will be better parents, workers, helpers and friends. We will suddenly realize that God is doing for us what we could not do for ourselves.

Are these extravagant promises? We think not. They are being fulfilled among us–sometimes quickly, sometimes slowly. They will always materialize if we work for them.

For those of you who are new to our fellowship, there are no problems that you have experienced that are not common to many of us.

Just as our love for our partners has been imperfect, we may not always be adequately able to express to you the deep love and acceptance we feel for you. Keep coming back; the process of loving and communication grows in us and with each other one day at a time.

From *Recovering Couples Anonymous*, 3rd Edition, page 59.

In Conclusion

Progress and miracles

Getting this far means that you have worked hard and given many gifts to yourselves. You have integrated 12-step principles into your core being and into the core of your relationship. You have changed the way you live your lives together dramatically, and you have a rich and growing community of friends. Let this workbook be a record of your transformation and a celebration of your courage and stamina.

Recovery as a couple, just like recovery from any unhealthy or dysfunctional behavior, is a lifelong process. There is no "cure" that will allow you to automatically and immediately have a perfect relationship.

Couples, just like individuals, want to return to the state that feels "normal" to them. This means that whatever behaviors and ways of relating you were taught as children seem normal to you as adults, however unhealthy they may be. Whatever behaviors have been routine in your relationship will feel safer to you than new behaviors. Changes in your lives and relationship, even though they may be healthy ones, may still seem frightening and abnormal. That's because you are not used to them. You don't know where they will lead or what they will mean in the long run. The return to the "normal" is known as relapse or a slip.

Symptoms of relapse may be familiar to you, and are commonly signaled by an experience of emotional and spiritual distance from one another. Your communication and recreation time may decrease. Your spiritual quest contract may be neglected. You also may feel increased anger and resentment toward each other. In short, many, if not all, the old unhealthy behaviors of your past may surface again.

Be gentle with yourselves if this happens. Many couples have experienced relapse or slips. Relapse can be educational; it can remind you of what your life used to be like, and it can prod you to take your recovery more seriously. Use slips or relapse as a reminder of what you still need to work on.

Be especially aware that after having worked these Twelve Steps for several weeks or months, you may be tempted to believe that you've got the system figured out. This is sometimes referred to as the "honeymoon effect." Remarkable improvements in your relationship seem to have taken place because of the tremendous energy you've used in your efforts to make your relationship better. You may be sorely tempted to think your relationship is well, that there's nothing left to do. Don't be fooled.

Relationships aren't static; they don't run smoothly without maintenance. You may find, for example, that you experience cyclical periods of stress in your life, and during those times you may be tempted to return to your old ways of coping, either individually or as a couple. Another sign of relapse can be a return to old addictive behaviors by one or both partners. Beware of these, and remember that they offer proof as to why you need to stay on your new, healthier path.

Finally, implementing changes and sticking with them until they feel normal takes practice–sometimes lots of practice. It can take months or years for the peace and serenity you seek to be the dominant force in your relationship.

There may come a time when you feel the need to revitalize your commitment to this process. You may wish to complete this workbook again. Many couples have related that using these exercises at different times in their lives generated very different experiences. Feel free to repeat them. All you need is the desire, the courage and some blank sheets of paper.

By now you've probably realized that there is no finish line on this gentle path through these Twelve Steps. The Steps are a process, ongoing, regenerating, renewing. There are always new challenges, and you will find, if you keep reaching out, plenty of friends along the way.

Our congratulations!

Patrick Carnes

Debra Laaser

Mark Laaser

Resources

Following is a list of recovery fellowships that may be helpful in your particular situation.

Adult Children of Alcoholics
310-534-1815
www.adultchildren.org

Alateen (age 12-17)
800-356-9996
www.al-anon-alateen.org

Al-Anon
800-344-2666
www.al-anon-alateen.org

Alcoholics Anonymous
212-870-3400
www.alcoholics-anonymous.org

Co-Dependents Anonymous
602-277-7991
www.ourcoda.com

Co-Dependents of Sex Addicts
612-537-6904

Cocaine Anonymous
800-347-8998
www.ca.org

CoAnon
www.co-anon.org

Debtors Anonymous
781-453-2743
www.debtorsanonymous.org

Emotions Anonymous
651-647-9712
www.mtn.org/EA

Families Anonymous
310-815-8010
www.familiesanonymous.org

Gamblers Anonymous
213-386-8789
www.gamblersanonymous.org

Marijuana Anonymous
212-459-4423
www.marijuana-anonymous.org

Narcotics Anonymous
818-773-9999
www.wsoirc.com

National Council for Couple and Family Recovery
314-997-9808

Nicotine Anonymous
516-348-2224

Overeaters Anonymous
www.oa.org

Recovering Couples Anonymous
314-830-2600

Recovery Online
www.recovery.alano.org

Runaway and Suicide Hotline
800-621-4000

S-Anon
615-833-3152

Sex & Love Addicts Anonymous
781-255-8825

Sex Addicts Anonymous
713-869-4902
www.sexaa.org

Sexual Compulsives Anonymous
310-859-5585

Survivors of Incest Anonymous
651-698-4177

More Gentle Path Press titles of related interest

BOOKS

The Betrayal Bond: Breaking Free of Exploitive Relationships
By Patrick Carnes, Ph.D.
Softbound

In a savage psychic twist, victims of abuse and violence often bond with their perpetrators to the stunning point that they will die rather than escape. Carnes' breakthrough book focuses on how betrayal intensifies trauma and illuminates the keys to escaping destructive relationships.

Sexual Anorexia: Overcoming Sexual Self-Hatred
By Patrick Carnes, Ph.D., with Joseph Moriarity
Softbound

The devastating mix of fear, pain and betrayal can lead to obsessive sexual aversion. Tracing the dysfunction's roots in childhood sexual trauma, neglect and abuse, Carnes explores dimensions of sexual health, targeting key issues that let recovery proceed.

Out of the Shadows: Understanding Sexual Addiction
By Patrick Carnes, Ph.D.
Softbound

The groundbreaking book that first identified and defined sexual addiction. A must for anyone looking to understand the illness, it's an expert and in-depth look at the origins of sexual addiction and the addiction cycle.

Contrary to Love: Helping the Sexual Addict
By Patrick Carnes, Ph.D.
Softbound

This sequel to *Out of the Shadows* traces the origins and consequences of the addict's faulty core beliefs. Building upon his earlier work, Carnes describes the stages of the illness and lays the groundwork for potential recovery.

Don't Call It Love: Recovering From Sexual Addiction
By Patrick Carnes, Ph.D.
Hardcover

This landmark study of 1,000 recovering sex addicts and their families explores how people become sex addicts and the role of culture, family, neurochemistry and child abuse in creating addiction.

A Gentle Path Through the Twelve Steps
By Patrick Carnes, Ph.D.
Softbound

A guidebook for people in recovery that helps them understand their own story and begin planning a new life of recovery. With more than 250,000 copies sold, it holds invaluable insights for beginners and old-timers alike in any 12-step program.

VIDEOTAPES

Trauma Bonds: When Humans Bond With Those Who Hurt Them
   Victims often cling to destructive relationships with baffling desperation. In this riveting videotape, Dr. Patrick Carnes analyzes how such trauma bonding develops and outlines strategies for breaking free from its compulsive torment.

Addiction Interaction Disorder: Understanding Multiple Addictions
   Few addicts–about 17 percent–have only one addiction. More commonly, assorted compulsions combine in a complex systemic problem called addiction interaction disorder. This tape outlines how to screen for the disorder (a major factor in relapse) and explores the role of addiction as a "solution" to trauma.

Contrary to Love: Helping the Sexual Addict
   A 12-part PBS video in which noted addiction psychologist Dr. Patrick Carnes discusses the spectrum of compulsive/addictive behavior and its treatment.
   Our Addictive Society
   Cultural Denial of Addiction
   Am I an Addict?
   Interview With Three
   The Addictive Family
   Interview With Melody Beattie
   Child Abuse
   The Twelve-Step Recovery Process
   Healthy Sexuality and Spirituality
   Finding a Balance in Recovery
   Coping in a World of Shame
   The Ten Risks of Recovery

AUDIOCASSETTES

Trauma Bonds: When We Bond to Those Who Hurt Us
Addiction Interaction Disorder: Understanding Multiple Addictions
Toward a New Freedom: Discovering Healthy Sexuality
Sexual Abuse in the Church
Sexual Dependency, Compulsion and Obsession
Signs of Sexual Addiction

At Gentle Path Press, our goal is to create and offer resources for recovery. We help the addicts who suffer, their loved ones who seek solace and the clinicians who bring hope and healing. An outgrowth of the visionary work of renowned addiction psychologist Patrick Carnes, Gentle Path offers books, videotapes, audiocassettes, software and more.

We appreciate you as our customer, strive to earn your continued support and look forward to your feedback.

Join us in a gentle path to recovery. Ask your local bookstore about our line of materials. View our complete catalog at www.gentlepath.com. Or contact us for a free catalog:

Gentle Path

P R E S S

P.O. Box 3345
Wickenburg, Arizona 85358
800-955-9853 (toll-free)

For Further Reading

The following list contains a bibliography of books mentioned, plus some further readings which may be helpful.

Co-Sex Addiction Recovery

Adult Children: The Secrets of Dysfunctional Families. John Friel and Linda Friel. Deerfield Beach: Health Communications, Inc., 1988.

Back From Betrayal: Recovering From His Affairs. Jennifer Schneider. New York: Ballantine Books, 1990.

Codependent No More: How to Stop Controlling Others and Start Caring for Yourself. Melody Beattie. New York: Walker & Company, 1989.

Facing Shame: Families in Recovery. Merle A. Fossum and Marilyn J. Mason. New York: W.W. Norton & Company, 1989.

Is It Love or Is It Addiction. Brenda Schaeffer. Fine Communications, 1995.

Sex, Lies and Forgiveness: Couples Speaking Out on Healing From Sex Addiction. Jennifer P. Schneider and Burt Schneider. Hazelden Information and Educational Services, 1991.

The Betrayal Bond: Breaking Free of Exploitive Relationships. Patrick J. Carnes. Deerfield Beach: Health Communications, Inc., 1998.

The Couple Who Became Each Other and Other Tales of Healing of a Master Hypnotherapist. David L. Calof and Robin Simons. Bantam Books, 1996.

Family

Bradshaw on the Family: A Revolutionary Way of Self-Discovery. John Bradshaw. Pompano Beach: Health Communications, 1988.

Emotional Incest Syndrome: What to Do When a Parent's Love Rules Your Life. Patricia Love. Bantam Books, 1991.

Facing Co-Dependency. Pia Mellody with Andrea Well Miller and J. Keith Miller. San Francisco: Harper San Francisco, 1989.

Family Secrets, What You Don't Know Can Hurt You. John Bradshaw. Bantam Books, 1996.

The Verbally Abusive Relationship: How to Recognize It and How to Respond. Patricia Evans. Holbrook: Adams Media Corporation, 1996.

Key Recovery Works

Craving for Ecstasy: The Chemistry and Consciousness of Escape. Harvey B. Milkman and Stanley Sunderwirth. New York: Free Press, 1987.

First Things First: Everyday. Stephen R. Covey. New York: Simon & Schuster, 1999.

Healing the Shame That Binds You. John Bradshaw. Deerfield Beach: Health Communications, Inc. 1988.

Hope and Recovery: The Twelve-Step Guide For Healing From Compulsive Sexual Behavior. Center City: Hazelden Educational Materials.

How to Get Out of Debt, Stay Out of Debt & Live Prosperously. Jerrold Mundis. Bantam Books, 1990.

Journey to the Heart: Daily Meditations on the Path to Freeing Your Soul. Melody Beattie.
    San Francisco: Harper San Francisco, 1996.
People of the Lie: The Hope for Healing Human Evil. M. Scott Peck. New York: Simon & Schuster,
    1985.
Reaching Out: The Three Movements of the Spiritual Life. Henri J. Nouwen. Garden City:
    Doubleday, 1986.
The Artist's Way: A Spiritual Path to Higher Creativity. Julia Cameron. New York: The Putnam
    Publishing Group, 1995.
The Money Drunk: Ninety Days to Financial Sobriety. Mark Bryan and Julia Cameron. New York:
    Ballantine Books, 1993.
*The Paradigm Conspiracy: How Our Systems of Government, School and Culture Violate Our Human
    Potential.* Denise Breton and Christopher Largent. Hazelden Information and Educational
    Services, 1998.
The Road Less Traveled. M. Scott Peck. New York: Simon & Schuster, 1978.
The Seven Habits of Highly Effective People: Powerful Lessons in Personal Change. Stephen R. Covey.
    New York: Simon & Schuster, 1989.
Way of the Peaceful Warrior: A Book That Changes Lives. Dan Millman. Tiburon: H.J. Kramer, Inc.,
    1984.

Sex Addiction

Answers in the Heart. San Francisco: Harper San Francisco, 1989.
Erotic Justice, A Liberating Ethic of Sexuality. Marvin M. Ellison. Louisville: Westminster John Knox
    Press, 1996.
From Generation to Generation: Learning About Adults Who Are Sexual With Children. Anne S.
    Hastings. Tiburon: The Printed Voice, 1994.
*Lonely All the Time: Recognizing, Understanding and Overcoming Sex Addiction, for Addicts and Co-
    Dependents.* Ralph H. Earle and Gregory Crowe. Bradt Publications, 1998.
Silently Seduced: When Parents Make Their Children Partners. Kenneth M. Adams. Deerfield Beach:
    Health Communications, Inc., 1991.
The Return of the Prodigal Son: A Story of Homecoming. Henri J. Nouwen. Doubleday, 1994.
Women, Sex and Addiction. Charlotte Kasl. Harper & Row Publishers, 1989.

Sexual Health

Aching for Love: The Sexual Drama of the Adult Child. Mary A. Klausner and Bobbie Hasselbring.
    San Francisco: Harper San Francisco, 1990.
Awakening Your Sexuality: A Recovery Guide for Women. Stephanie Covington. San Francisco:
    Harper San Francisco, 1991.
*Discovering Sexuality That Will Satisfy You Both: When Couples Want Differing Amounts and Different
    Kinds of Sex.* Anne S. Hastings. Tiburon: The Printed Voice, 1993.
Male Menopause: Sex and Survival in the Second Half of Life. Jed Diamond. Naperville:
    Sourcebooks, Inc., 1997.
Passionate Hearts: The Poetry of Sexual Love. Wendy Maltz, editor. Novato: New World Library,
    1997.
Positively Gay. Betty Berzon, editor. Berkeley: CelestialArts, 1995.

Seven Weeks to Better Sex. Domeena Renshaw. New York: Random House, 1995.

The Chalice and the Blade: Our History, Our Future. Riane Eisler. San Francisco: Harper & Row, Publishers, 1987.

The Practical Encyclopedia of Sex and Health. Stephen Bechtal. Rodale Press, 1993.

The Sexual Healing Journey: A Guide for Survivors of Sexual Abuse. Wendy Maltz. New York: HarperCollins Publishers, Inc., 1991.

Sex and Religion

A Gospel of Shame: Children, Sexual Abuse and the Catholic Church. Elinor Burkett and Frank Bruni. New York: Viking Penguin, 1993.

A Tragic Grace: The Catholic Church and Child Sexual Abuse. Stephen J. Rossetti. Collegeville: The Liturgical Press, 1996.

Faithful and True. Mark Laaser. Zondervan.

Restoring the Soul of a Church: Reconciling Congregations Wounded by Clergy Sexual Misconduct. Mark Laaser, editor. Collegeville: The Liturgical Press, 1995.

Sex, Priests and Power: Anatomy of a Crisis. A.W. Richard Sipe. New York: Brunner/Mazel Publishers, 1995.

Trauma Resolution

Abused Boys: The Neglected Victims of Sexual Abuse. Mic Hunter. New York: Fawcett Book Group, 1991.

Allies in Healing: When the Person You Love Was Sexually Abused as a Child. Laura Davis. HarperCollins, 1991.

Facing Shame: Families in Recovery. Merle A. Fossum and Marilyn J. Mason. New York: W.W. Norton & Company, 1986.

For Your Own Good: Hidden Cruelty in Child-Rearing and the Roots of Violence. Alice Miller. New York: Farrar, Straus, Giroux, 1990.

Healing the Incest Wound: Adult Survivors in Therapy. Christine A. Courtois. New York: W.W. Norton & Company, 1996.

Incest and Sexuality: A Guide to Understanding and Healing. Wendy Maltz and Beverly Holman. Lexington: Lexington Books, 1987.

Opening the Door: A Treatment Model for Therapy With Male Survivors of Sexual Abuse. Adrienne Crowder. Philadelphia: Brunner/Mazel Publishers, 1995.

Resolving Sexual Abuse: Solution-Focused Therapy and Ericksonian Hypnosis for Adult Survivors. Yvonne Dolan. New York: W W Norton & Company, 1991.

The Courage to Heal: A Guide for Women Survivors of Child Sexual Abuse. Ellen Bass and Laura Davis. New York: HarperCollins, 1994.

The Incestuous Workplace: Stress and Distress in the Organizational Family. William L. White. Hazelden Information and Educational Services, 1997.

Trauma and Recovery: The Aftermath of Violence from Domestic Abuse to Political Terror. Judith Lewis Herman. Basic Books, 1992.

Traumatic Stress: The Effects of Overwhelming Experience on Mind, Body and Society. Bessel A. Van der Kolk, editor. The Guilford Press Publications, 1996.

About the Authors

Patrick Carnes, Ph.D., CAS, is a nationally known trainer and speaker on addiction and recovery issues, as well as the author of seven books on addiction and recovery. Dr. Carnes was the focus of the 12-part PBS show *Contrary to Love*, the well-known series on addiction issues. He is clinical director for sexual disorders services at The Meadows Institute in Wickenburg, Arizona, where he designed programs for sexual addiction and trauma treatment. The educational and therapeutic services for sexual disorders available at The Meadows are built on the technology evolved through Dr. Carnes' landmark study of the recoveries of 1,000 sex addicts. This work, summarized in *Don't Call It Love*, has been described as the best book available about addiction and its consequences.

Dr. Carnes is the father of four children and has two dogs, Slick and Sallie. He resides with his wife, Suzanne, in Wickenburg, Arizona. He loves to hunt, fish and restore antique and classic outboard motors.

Debra Laaser is the president and CEO of Yours, Mine and Ours, Inc., an international company that produces watercolor drawings for the gift industry. She is an avid tennis player and golfer.

Mark Laaser, Ph.D., CAS, is an author of several books, including *Faithful and True*, *Before the Fall* and *Talking to Your Children About Sex*, and is a speaker and workshop leader. He also attempts tennis and golf and is trying to remodel a home.

Married for over 25 years, Mark and Deb are the parents of Sarah, Jon and Ben, and are currently trying to let go of all of them. They have led couples workshops and tried to practice what they preach since 1987.

We'd Like to Hear From You!

Books can become evolving documents through reader feedback. The authors and NCCFR welcome your suggestions, contributions and criticisms. Please contact us at Gentle Path Press, P.O. Box 3345, Wickenburg, AZ 85358. Or email us at info@gentlepath.com.

List of Exercises